Perspectives in Law, Business and Innovation

Over the last three decades, interconnected processes of globalization and rapid technological change—particularly, the emergence of networked technologies—have profoundly disrupted traditional models of business organization. This economic transformation has created multiple new opportunities for the emergence of alternate business forms, and disruptive innovation has become one of the major driving forces in the contemporary economy. Moreover, in the context of globalization, the innovation space increasingly takes on a global character. The main stakeholders—innovators, entrepreneurs and investors—now have an unprecedented degree of mobility in pursuing economic opportunities wherever they arise. As such, frictionless movement of goods, workers, services, and capital is becoming the "new normal".

This new economic and social reality has created multiple regulatory challenges for policymakers as they struggle to come to terms with the rapid pace of these social and economic changes. Moreover, these challenges impact across multiple fields of both public and private law. Nevertheless, existing approaches within legal science often struggle to deal with innovation and its effects.

Paralleling this shift in the economy, we can, therefore, see a similar process of disruption occurring within contemporary academia, as traditional approaches and disciplinary boundaries—both within and between disciplines—are being re-configured. Conventional notions of legal science are becoming increasingly obsolete or, at least, there is a need to develop alternative perspectives on the various regulatory challenges that are currently being created by the new innovation-driven global economy.

The aim of this series is to provide a forum for the publication of cutting-edge research in the fields of innovation and the law from a Japanese and Asian perspective. The series will cut across the traditional sub-disciplines of legal studies but will be tied together by a focus on contemporary developments in an innovation-driven economy and will deepen our understanding of the various regulatory responses to these economic and social changes.

The series editor and editorial board carefully assess each book proposal and sample chapters in terms of their relevance to law, business, and innovative technological change. Each proposal is evaluated on the basis of its academic value and distinctive contribution to the fast-moving debate in these fields.

All books and chapters in the Perspectives in Law, Business and Innovation book series are indexed in Scopus.

Iana Kazeeva

Sui Generis Intellectual Property Protection

Comparison of EU and U.S. Regulatory Approaches

Springer

Iana Kazeeva
Department of Innovation
and Digitalisation in Law
University of Vienna
Vienna, Austria

ISSN 2520-1875 ISSN 2520-1883 (electronic)
Perspectives in Law, Business and Innovation
ISBN 978-981-99-8896-9 ISBN 978-981-99-8897-6 (eBook)
https://doi.org/10.1007/978-981-99-8897-6

This Springer imprint is published by the registered company Springer Nature Singapore Pte Ltd.
The registered company address is: 152 Beach Road, #21-01/04 Gateway East, Singapore 189721, Singapore

To my husband and son.

Preface

The standard forms of intellectual property protection, namely copyright, patents, trademarks and trade secrets, have a long history and are well regulated in the legislative systems of most jurisdictions. However, there are specific kinds of subject matter that, due to their characteristics, cannot be adequately protected by these standard forms of intellectual property instruments. At the same time, these categories of subject matter require legal protection in order to ensure the balance between the public's access to these creations and the creators' rights. For these reasons, many jurisdictions introduce special forms of intellectual property protection, namely *sui generis* regimes.

As used in this volume, the term "*sui generis* rights" refers to intellectual property rights used for protection of specific subject matter and different from the traditional forms of intellectual property rights (copyright, trademarks, patent, trade secret), thus reflecting the literal meaning of the Latin term ("of its own kind").

The purpose of this book is to examine the nature of, and the rationale for, *sui generis* intellectual property protection and, based on case studies of three categories of subject matter (databases, designs and plant varieties), to determine whether granting *sui generis* rights is the optimal solution to provide legal protection for the analyzed categories of subject matter. The final chapter of this book aims to evaluate the perspectives of introducing a *sui generis* regime for the protection of works generated by AI systems.

There have been a number of research projects examining the question of whether *sui generis* intellectual property protection should be granted for specific categories of subject matter. For instance, Suthersanen analyzed the case of utility model *sui generis* laws by way of examining the theoretical justifications for providing an alternative *sui generis* regime, as well as by looking at national case studies, particularly the examples of Japan and Australia.[1] Goldstein examined the use of a *sui*

[1] See Uma Suthersanen 'Utility models: do they really serve national innovation strategies?' in Josef Drexl and Anselm Kamperman Sanders (eds) *The Innovation Society and Intellectual Property* (Edward Elgar 2019) 2 <https://www.elgaronline.com/view/edcoll/9781789902341/9781789902341.00010.xml> accessed 12 January 2022.

generis regime for the protection of compilations of data, focusing on the practical aspects of the *sui generis* system for businesses.[2] Bizer, Lankau, Spindler und Zimbehl analyzed the economic and political implications of *sui generis* rights for the protection of traditional cultural expressions, evaluating economic effects that can be expected to result from these regulatory alternatives.[3] Phillips described the current dissatisfaction with the protection for computer software by copyright law and discussed the alternative *sui generis* protection, proposing a legislative program for the protection of computer software.[4] Correa provided a detailed history of the *sui generis* rights for plant varieties and focused on the peculiarities of these rights in India, Thailand and Malaysia.[5]

However, there has been little comparative study of *sui generis* intellectual property protection that would evaluate the effectiveness of *sui generis* regimes and estimate whether the goals pursued by the legislators introducing *sui generis* regimes for different kinds of subject matter have been achieved. Thus, this book is aimed at filling this gap and contributing to a better understanding of *sui generis* intellectual property rights.

This book is divided into five chapters. The first chapter will introduce the problem of *sui generis* intellectual property protection and will examine the nature of, and the reasons for, emerging of *sui generis* intellectual property rights. This chapter opens with examining the concept of intellectual property and describing the various rationales for intellectual property legal protection. A description of development of intellectual property over time and its extension to new subject matter will follow. Such summary of the theoretical basics of intellectual property, including the economic, social, and political rationales behind it, is crucial for understanding the reasons why new forms of intellectual property emerge. This chapter further demonstrates why the standard forms of intellectual property legal protection are sometimes not enough to protect certain categories of subject matter, which triggers introduction of *sui generis* rights. In its final part, this chapter will examine how the *sui generis* rights fit into the intellectual property legal framework.

The following three chapters of this volume include three case studies of how the EU and the U.S. extended intellectual property protection to the subject matter that is often considered as requiring *sui generis* protection. Particularly, these chapters will analyze, in turn, the legal regulation of databases, designs and plant varieties

---

[2] Bruce Goldstein, 'Sui Generis: A Unique Form of Intellectual Property Governing Compilations of Data' (2010) 3 AUTM Technology Transfer Practice Manual <https://www.autm.net/AUTMMain/media/ThirdEditionPDFs/V3/TTP_V3_P3_SuiGeneris.pdf> accessed 27 October 2022.

[3] Kilian Bizer, Matthias Lankau, Gerald Spindler und Philipp Zimbehl, 'Sui Generis Rights for the Protection of Traditional Cultural Expressions: Policy Implications' in Kilian Bizer, Matthias Lankau und Gerald Spindler (eds) *Sui generis Rechte zum Schutz traditioneller kultureller Ausdrucksweisen* (Göttingen University Press 2017) 131.

[4] John C. Phillips, 'Sui Generis Intellectual Property Protection for Computer Software' (1992) George Washington Law Review, Note, April 1992 <https://cyber.harvard.edu/property/protection/resources/phillips_unedited.html> accessed 27 October 2022.

[5] Carlos M. Correa, 'Sui generis protection for farmers' varieties' in Michael Halewood (ed) *Farmers' Crop Varieties and Farmers' Rights. Challenges in Taxonomy and Law* (Routledge 2016).

in the EU and U.S. The three categories of protectable subject matter have been chosen so as to represent three different areas of creations of the human intellect: physical compilations of data and digital technologies (databases), creative ideas (designs) and plant biology (plant varieties). The primary objective of these chapters is to determine whether the granting of *sui generis* intellectual property rights for the analyzed categories of subject matter has proved to be effective over time, particularly whether the special regulation introduced in these jurisdictions has helped achieve the goals pursued by the legislators in the respective jurisdictions.

The fifth chapter of this book will examine the question whether works generated by AI systems should be protected by a specially created intellectual property right, i.e., a *sui generis* regime. In order to answer this question, this chapter will look into the phenomenon of artificial intelligence, its differences from human intelligence and will analyze, through the lens of intellectual property law theories, which forms of intellectual property protection are most suitable for AI outputs.

Finally, this book will draw the conclusions on the application of *sui generis* intellectual property protection for the analyzed areas in the EU and U.S. Based on the conducted analysis for the three categories of subject matter, this chapter will conclude whether the *sui generis* regimes in each of the three areas have proved to be successful and will elaborate on the reasons behind it, taking into consideration the different economic, territorial and political factors. In particular, as will be demonstrated throughout this book, *sui generis* regimes prove to be more effective when introduced as specific, supranational forms of protection. However, they do not guarantee enhancing innovation or investments in the protected subject matter. As to *sui generis* regime for AI-generated works, such a regime may be justifiable if aimed at protection of investments into AI systems, which is still subject to empirical economic evidence.

Vienna, Austria Iana Kazeeva

About the Author

Iana Kazeeva is a postdoctoral researcher at the Department of Innovation and Digitalisation in Law at the Faculty of Law of the University of Vienna. She studied international commercial and tax law in Moscow and holds a Candidate of Sciences degree (Ph.D. equivalent) in international financial law (dissertation on fiscal decentralization). She has an LL.M. degree in European and International Business Law from the University of Vienna and completed the U.S. intellectual property law certificate program at Stanford University. Prior to joining the Department, she worked at the Mountain View office of a California-based media technology company, primarily engaged in reviewing and negotiating technology and commercial contracts. She also gained practical experience as a senior legal counsel at the legal department of a global producer of mineral fertilizers based in Moscow, focusing on project finance and legal compliance. Her academic research interests include intellectual property, international contract and data protection law.

Contents

Abbreviations

AI	Artificial Intelligence
AIPPI	International Association for the Protection of Intellectual Property
BIRPI	United International Bureaux for the Protection of Intellectual Property
CJEU	Court of Justice of the European Union
CPVR	Community Plant Variety Right
DPPA	Design Piracy Prohibition Act
ECJ	European Court of Justice
EPC	European Patent Convention
EPO	European Patent Office
EU	European Union
IDPA	Innovative Design Protection Act
IDPPPA	Innovative Design Protection and Piracy Prevention Act
ISF	International Seed Federation
PPA	Plant Patent Act
PVPA	Plant Variety Protection Act
PVPO	Plant Variety Protection Office
RCD	Registered Community Design
TRIPS	Agreement on Trade-Related Aspects of Intellectual Property Rights
U.S.	United States of America
UCD	Unregistered Community Design
UPOV	International Union for the Protection of New Varieties of Plants
USPTO	United States Patent and Trademark Office
VHDPA	Vessel Hull Design Protection Act
WIPO	World Intellectual Property Organization.

Chapter 1
Sui Generis Rights in the Intellectual Property System

1.1 Intellectual Property: Overview

Intellectual property plays a crucial role in the modern information economy, being one of the most common and frequently used systems of encouraging and protecting ideas and innovations. Intellectual property is not a novel concept, one of the first references to intellectual property protection dating back to ancient Greece.[1] Over the years, the system of intellectual property regimes matured, covering different categories of subject matter, whereas several justifications were offered for intellectual property protection. Widely recognized are the four main theories: the utilitarian (incentive) theory, labor theory of property, personality theory of property, and the less-recognized social planning theory.[2]

The incentive theory is the predominant philosophical foundation for intellectual property legal protection in the U.S. Under the incentive theory, the grant of intellectual property rights is viewed as a reward (incentive) system designed to encourage creativity and innovations. Without such incentive, a person might not invest the time, money, and energy into creating new works, or would not have the incentive to disclose inventions to the public, because such works or inventions might be copied cheaply and easily, eliminating the authors' or inventors' ability to profit from their works or inventions.[3] Such utilitarian argument is supported by the U.S. Constitution, empowering Congress "to promote the progress of science and useful arts,

---

[1] Stanford Encyclopedia of Philosophy. Intellectual Property <https://plato.stanford.edu/entries/intellectual-property/> accessed 7 January 2022.

[2] William Fisher, 'Theories of Intellectual Property' in Stephen Munzer (ed), *New Essays in the Legal and Political Theory of Property* (Cambridge University Press 2001) <https://cyber.harvard.edu/people/tfisher/iptheory.pdf> accessed 30 December 2021.

[3] Jeanne C. Fromer, 'Expressive Incentives in Intellectual Property' (2012) 98 Virginia Law Review <https://law.stanford.edu/wp-content/uploads/sites/default/files/event/265497/media/slspublic/Expressive_Incentives_in_Intellectual_Property_1.pdf> accessed 2 January 2022.

I. Kazeeva, *Sui Generis Intellectual Property Protection*, Perspectives in Law, Business and Innovation, https://doi.org/10.1007/978-981-99-8897-6_1

by securing for limited times to authors and inventors the exclusive right to their respective writings and discoveries".[4]

The labor theory of property is predominant in the EU and is based on Locke's appropriation theory formulated in Chapter V, Book II of the "Two Treatises of Government" (1690). Under this theory, resources are common, but a person owns his or her body and the labor produced by it. Mixing one's labor with resources found in the common gives rise to property rights.[5] As well known, the main concept of Locke's second Treatise was to undermine the idea of absolutist monarchical government, and thus the labor theory of property just played a supporting role in proving that monarchs could not claim complete authority over the world as ascertained by Filmer in his "Patriarcha: or the Natural Power of Kings" (1680).[6] However, Locke's appropriation theory is widely used to explain the notion of, and the rationale for, intellectual property. Thus, under Locke's theory, an individual creator, by annexing labor and efforts to the "raw material" supplied by the public domain, becomes the owner of the creation.

The personality theory of property is derived from the writings of Kant and Hegel. Kant believed that any object onto which a person projects his or her will may be owned and that people naturally want to project their will on objects they find in the world.[7] In Hegel's "Philosophy of Right" (1821), the central concept is the concept of will, which a person has the right to put in any and every thing, thus making property the embodiment of personality.[8] From this standpoint, intellectual property is the extension and embodiment of authors' or inventors' will and personality.

The labor and the personality theories of property are sometimes seen as two flavors of natural rights theories, i.e., theories grounded in the natural rights that authors and inventors deserve by virtue of having created their works.[9]

The fourth rationale, referred to by Fisher as "social planning theory", is based on the idea that intellectual property rights should be designed in a way to foster a "just and attractive culture". This approach, however, is less established than the three rationales described above and is not widely recognized.[10]

As Moore writes, intellectual property is generally characterized as non-physical property that is the product of cognitive processes, the value of which is based upon

---

[4] U.S. Constitution Article I § 8 Clause 8.

[5] Robert P. Merges, 'Justifying Intellectual Property' (Harvard University Press 2011) 34–35.

[6] Peter Drahos, 'A Philosophy of Intellectual Property' (ANU eText) <https://press-files.anu.edu.au/downloads/press/n1902/html/ch03.xhtml#footnote-219> accessed 28 December 2021.

[7] Robert P. Merges, 'Justifying Intellectual Property' (Harvard University Press 2011) 72–74.

[8] Peter Drahos, 'A Philosophy of Intellectual Property' (ANU eText) <https://press-files.anu.edu.au/downloads/press/n1902/html/ch03.xhtml#footnote-219> accessed 28 December 2021.

[9] Jeanne C. Fromer, 'Expressive Incentives in Intellectual Property' (2012) 98 Virginia Law Review <https://law.stanford.edu/wp-content/uploads/sites/default/files/event/265497/media/slspublic/Expressive_Incentives_in_Intellectual_Property_1.pdf> accessed 2 January 2022.

[10] William Fisher, 'Theories of Intellectual Property' in Stephen Munzer (ed), *New Essays in the Legal and Political Theory of Property* (Cambridge University Press 2001) <https://cyber.harvard.edu/people/tfisher/iptheory.pdf> accessed 30 December 2021.

some idea or collection of ideas.[11] However, the legal notion of intellectual property has not always been as it is today and has been gradually evolving over time, with the advancement of technology and the global economy. Particularly, the term was traditionally used to refer to copyright protection of authors and to distinguish it from industrial property (patents, trademarks, industrial design rights, etc.).[12]

However, nowadays, intellectual property is the term used to describe the legal regimes that assign limited exclusive rights to inventions, creations, trademarks, designs, and trade secrets.[13] Fisher offers an even broader definition of intellectual property saying that it is a "loose cluster of legal doctrines that regulate the uses of different sorts of ideas and insignia".[14] In other words, the term "intellectual property" is now used as a generic term encompassing copyright, patents, trademarks, trade secrets, and other forms of legal protection. A common characteristic of these intellectual property rights is that individuals acquire power to stop others from engaging in commercial conduct of a particular kind.[15]

As used in the TRIPS Agreement, the term "intellectual property" refers to the seven following subject matter categories: copyright and related rights, trademarks, geographical indications, industrial designs, patents, layout designs of integrated circuits, trade secret or confidential information (Article 1(2)).[16] Reichman writes that the eighth subject matter category is the control of anti-competitive practices in contractual licenses, presumably exempted from the national treatment and most favored nation principles applicable to the above mentioned seven forms of intellectual property protection (Articles 3 and 4). The TRIPS Agreement establishes minimum substantive standards for each of these intellectual property regimes.[17]

However, technology has enhanced opportunities for imitation, which has triggered the creation of new forms of intellectual property for newly emerging subject matter. As Cornish writes, intellectual property may be extended to new subject matter either by accretion or by emulation. In case of accretion, an existing intellectual property right is redefined so as to cover the novel subject matter, whereas in

---

[11] Adam D. Moore, 'A Lockean Theory of Intellectual Property' (1997) 21 Hamline Law Review 65, 67.

[12] William R. Cornish, 'The International Relations of Intellectual Property' (1993) 52(1) Cambridge Law Journal 46.

[13] Richard Gilbert, 'A World Without Intellectual Property? Boldrin and Levine, Against Intellectual Monopoly' (2011) 49 Journal of Economic Literature 421 <https://escholarship.org/uc/item/3h7363s3> accessed 3 January 2022.

[14] William Fisher, 'Theories of Intellectual Property' in Stephen Munzer (ed), *New Essays in the Legal and Political Theory of Property* (Cambridge University Press 2001) <https://cyber.harvard.edu/people/tfisher/iptheory.pdf> accessed 30 December 2021.

[15] William R. Cornish, 'The International Relations of Intellectual Property' (n 12).

[16] WTO. Agreement on Trade Related Aspects of Intellectual Property Rights, Including Trade in Counterfeit Goods <https://www.wto.org/english/docs_e/legal_e/27-trips_01_e.htm> accessed 4 January 2022.

[17] Jerome H. Reichman, 'Universal Minimum Standards of Intellectual Property Protection Under the TRIPS Component of the WTO Agreement' (1995) 29 International Lawyer 345, 348 <https://scholarship.law.duke.edu/cgi/viewcontent.cgi?article=1617&context=faculty_scholarship> accessed 4 January 2022.

case of emulation, a new right is created by analogy drawn from the existing intellectual property rights.[18] Cornish offers two illustrative examples of these two forms of extension of intellectual property protection. Thus, major computer lobbyists in the United States pressed for computer programs to be protected by accretion, i.e., by treating them as literary works within the concept of copyright; whereas for the design of semiconductor chips, they insisted on protection by emulation, i.e., creation of a *sui generis* right, which was finally stipulated in the 1984 Semiconductor Chip Protection Act.[19]

Besides the newly emerging objects for intellectual property protection, there are other categories of subject matter, such as designs or geographical indications, that have existed for centuries and, despite their long history, have not received as strong protection through the existing intellectual property regimes as other categories of subject matter. Some jurisdictions have acknowledged the need for a *sui generis* intellectual property regime for these kinds of subject matter, i.e., have opted for emulation, whereas other jurisdictions offer protection through the already existing regimes, i.e., by accretion.

The categories of subject matter that could not get adequate protection with the standard forms of intellectual property protection include databases, designs, and plant varieties. However, there is no affirmative answer whether granting *sui generis* intellectual property rights is the best way to address the gaps in legal protection for these categories of subject matter. In the following sections, this book will further examine the background of, and the reasons for, creation of special regimes of intellectual property protection, the notion of *sui generis* intellectual property rights and how the EU and the U.S. have dealt with providing legal protection for the chosen categories of subject matter.

1.2 The Reasons for *Sui Generis* Intellectual Property Protection

Although the legal concept of intellectual property has been developing over hundreds of years and its legal framework is well developed and includes multiple forms of legal protection, there are certain categories of subject matter that cannot be effectively protected by the existing intellectual property legal regimes. This is the case when the need for a *sui generis*, i.e., of its own kind, protection emerges. For instance, the purpose of early utility models laws was to protect functional improvements of handtools, which neither patent nor trade secret law effectively protected.[20] Besides filling such legal gaps, another reason for introducing *sui generis* regimes is derived

[18] William R. Cornish, 'The International Relations of Intellectual Property' (n 12).

[19] 98 Stat. 3335.

[20] Jerome H. Reichman, 'Legal Hybrids Between the Patent and Copyright Paradigms' [1994] *Columbia Law Review* 2432, 2456 <https://scholarship.law.duke.edu/faculty_scholarship/97/> accessed 2 November 2021.

from the utilitarian theory of intellectual property protection, namely, the need to find the balance between the public's access to inventions and creations, on the one hand, and the proprietors' interests, on the other hand.

The list of subject matter, for which the need for *sui generis* intellectual property protection has been either claimed for, or acknowledged, in a number of jurisdictions or at international level, includes databases, designs, plant varieties, semiconductor chips, geographical indications, traditional knowledge, etc.[21] Recently, the issue of granting *sui generis* protection for works generated by artificial intelligence models has also been raised by scholars and practitioners.[22] This book will further discuss the forms of intellectual property protection available for databases, designs, and plant varieties, representing three different areas of creations of the human intellect: physical compilations of data and digital technologies (databases), creative ideas (designs) and plant biology (plant varieties).

Databases and other compilations can generally be protected under copyright law, which is stipulated at both national and international levels. However, databases and compilations are often referred to as "low-authorship factual works",[23] which demonstrates the main legal problem that authors face when trying to get copyright protection for databases: lack of originality. Indeed, before the introduction of the *sui generis* protection for databases in the EU, only three among the fifteen EU Member States protected a significant number of databases using copyright, which was possible due to applying a very low threshold of originality.[24] Furthermore, the courts in the U.S.[25] and EU[26] confirmed that copyright law does not protect databases that result merely from economic investment or intellectual effort.

As to ornamental designs, which are in principle patentable in the U.S., in practice the process of getting a patent for such designs is too costly and slow for the fast-moving, short-lived products of mass consumption.[27] At the same time, copyright protection is in most countries strictly limited for ornamental designs. For example, in the U.S., clothing, furniture, dinnerware, etc., are considered useful articles having

---

[21] See, e.g., Susy Frankel and Daniel Gervais (eds), *The Internet and the Emerging Importance of New Forms of Intellectual Property* (Kluwer Law International 2016).

[22] See, e.g., Intellectual Property Owners Association. 'Sui Generis Rights for Trained AI Models' (2020) <https://ipo.org/wp-content/uploads/2020/11/SG-model-rights-committee-paper-pub.pdf > accessed 16 February 2023.

[23] See, e.g., Daniel J. Gervais, 'The Protection of Databases' (2007) 82 Chi.-Kent L. Rev. 1109; Graham Greenleaf and David Lindsay, 'Public Rights: Copyright's Public Domains' (Cambridge University Press 2018) 191; Jerome H. Reichman, 'Legal Hybrids Between the Patent and Copyright Paradigms' (n 20) 2490.

[24] Jens L. Gaster, 'The New EU Directive concerning the Legal Protection of Databases' (1996) 20 Fordham Int.L.J. 1129, 1141.

[25] See, e.g., *Feist Publications, Inc. v. Rural Telephone Service Co., Inc.* U.S. Supreme Court 111 S.Ct. 1282 (1991) (discussed in more detail in Part II of this volume).

[26] See, e.g., *Van Dale Lexicografie B.V. v. Rudolf Jan Romme* Supreme Court of the Netherlands NJ 1991/608 (1991) (discussed in more detail in Part II of this volume).

[27] Jerome H. Reichman, 'Legal Hybrids Between the Patent and Copyright Paradigms' (n 20) 2460.

intrinsic utilitarian functions, and, therefore, the design of these articles cannot be protected by copyright law.[28]

For innovations in the agricultural industry, trade secret and patent laws could be the appropriate instruments for legal protection. Use of trade secret laws for protection of genetic information in an inbred plant line was upheld in *Pioneer Hi-Bred International v. Holden Foundation Seed*,[29] despite the fact that parent plants are grown outdoors over a wide area, which contradicts the traditional trade secret law requirement to keep information secret. However, trade secret protection is only available for those crops that are sold as a hybrid seed, as opposed to self-pollinated crops, because in that case the parental plant lines can be kept secret.[30] Patent law does not provide full relief either, since the products of nature are generally excluded from patentable subject matter in the U.S.[31] The majority of the leading European countries are also reluctant to bring life forms within the domestic patent laws, at least for plants obtained through conventional breeding processes, since granting such patents could potentially lead to creation of monopolies and raise food prices.[32] The need for *sui generis* protection for plant varieties has also been recognized at the international level. Particularly, Article 27.3 of the TRIPS Agreement states that "members shall provide protection for plant varieties either by patents or by an effective sui generis system, or by any combination thereof".

Indeed, the mentioned categories of subject matter can be protected by a combination of the standard intellectual property regimes. For instance, an ornamental feature of a design can be protected by a design patent, by copyright as the author's expression, and by trademark law (in the form of a trade dress) as a source indicator. However, the overlapping rights make it difficult for intellectual property users to determine the scope of such different rights, particularly when those rights have different terms or limitations. In order to resolve this issue, some scholars suggested that courts should require intellectual property owners to choose the right they want enforced or follow the requirements of the regime whose protection term expires first. Besides, although the courts might not object to invoking overlapping intellectual property regimes as long as the requirements for each regime are met, it is not clear to what extent a particular intellectual property right should be enforced. Therefore,

---

[28] U.S. Copyright Office <https://www.copyright.gov/register/va-useful.html> accessed 5 November 2021.

[29] *Pioneer Hi-Bred International. Inc. v. Holden Foundation Seeds, Inc.* No. 81–60-E slip op. S.D. Iowa, Oct. 29, 1987.

[30] Nicholas S. Seay, 'Intellectual Property in Plants' in P. Stephen Baenziger, Roger A. Kleese, Robert F Barnes (eds), *Intellectual Property Rights: Protection of Plant Materials* 61, 66 (Crop Science Society of America 1993).

[31] 35 U.S.C. § 101.

[32] 'Parliament says no to patenting plants bred naturally' European Parliament, News, 23 September 2019 <https://www.europarl.europa.eu/news/en/headlines/society/20190912STO60951/parliament-says-no-to-patenting-plants-bred-naturally> accessed 22 November 2021.

such doctrinal overlap presents a temptation to intellectual property owners to push for even stronger protection of their intellectual property rights.[33]

Another possible instrument of protection is the unfair competition laws. However, unfair competition laws are a completely different legal concept and are applicable only in certain situations and therefore do not provide enough protection. In particular, the law of unfair competition is only applicable in competitive situations, whereas the *sui generis* right also covers acts committed in non-competitive situations. Besides, the law of unfair competition sanctions unfair behavior *a posteriori*, whereas the *sui generis* rights create rights *a priori* and grant a term of protection.[34]

Thus, the legal gaps in the existing intellectual property legal regimes prompt the creation of special legal regimes of protection of intellectual property. Usually created for specific categories of subject matter, such *sui generis* rights have been the subject of much controversy as to their legal nature and their place in the intellectual property legal framework, as will be discussed in further detail in the following section.

1.3 The Legal Nature of *Sui Generis* Rights

There are various views on the legal nature of *sui generis* intellectual property rights, which is clearly reflected in the variety of terms used to describe this legal concept.

Reichman refers to "legal hybrids between the patent and copyright paradigms".[35] He states that the international intellectual property system represents a bipolar framework of industrial property and literary and artistic property, based on the 1883 Paris Convention for the Protection of Industrial Property[36] and the Berne Convention for the Protection of Literary and Artistic Works.[37] The author represents the two classical intellectual property regimes graphically, with spectrum of protection ranging from "thick" (strong) to "thin" (weak) and meeting face to face at the line of demarcation. Patented inventions and traditional copyrighted works are conceptually located toward the outer ends of their respective spectra where the scope of protection is relatively "thick" (strong), whereas the deviant or marginal intellectual property models appear closer to the line of demarcation between industrial and artistic property, where the scope of protection is "thin" (weak). Reichman further provides examples of the deviant protective regimes on each side of the

[33] Laura A. Heymann, 'Overlapping Intellectual Property Doctrines: Election of Rights versus Selection of Remedies' (2013) 17 Stan. Tech. L. Rev. 239.

[34] See Jens L. Gaster, 'The New EU Directive concerning the Legal Protection of Databases' (n 24), as it applies to the *sui generis* right for the protection of databases in the EU. However, the same principles are applicable to other *sui generis* rights.

[35] Jerome H. Reichman, 'Legal Hybrids Between the Patent and Copyright Paradigms' (n 20).

[36] WIPO. Paris Convention for the Protection of Industrial Property <https://www.wipo.int/treaties/en/ip/paris/index.html> accessed 14 January 2022.

[37] Berne Convention for the Protection of Literary and Artistic Works (as amended on September 28, 1979) <https://wipolex.wipo.int/en/treaties/textdetails/12214> accessed 22 November 2021.

line. Particularly, utility model laws, registered and unregistered design laws, plant variety protection laws are located on the industrial property side. In the spectrum of artistic property, there are *sui generis* regimes protecting computer programs, databases and catalogues, laws on protection of non-functional appearance designs in France, and related rights (protecting performers, producers of sound recordings, and broadcasting organizations).

Suthersanen points out that *sui generis* intellectual property rights emanate from the inability of legislators and jurists to stretch the existing instruments of the intellectual property regime to accommodate new things to protect. Although *sui generis* rights incorporate an "ad hoc mixture of copyright, patent or trade mark principles", it would be not correct to suggest that they are merely derivative instruments of the standard instruments of intellectual property protection that we use today. In fact, Suthersanen notes that some of the *sui generis* intellectual property rights have had long legislative histories and previously played important roles in textile industry, agriculture, mechanical product industries, as the modern notion of intellectual property was slowly evolving. Some of the early examples of *sui generis* intellectual property rights include the laws on protection of academic compilations in Prussia, regulations protecting geographical indications in China, etc.[38]

Janis examines the so-called "second tier protection regime" in patent laws, also known as "utility model" or "petty patent", arguing that such regimes do not find a solid foundation in either history or policy. The author claims that there is no satisfactory economic justification for awarding legal protection to "subpatentable" innovations. Although some subject matter may be unprotected, Janis suggests that the effort should be directed towards reforming regular patent laws instead.[39] Interestingly, this turned out to be the case for the proposed *sui generis* utility model regime in the EU. The European Commission's proposal for a directive on the protection of utility models presented in 1997 was suspended in 2000 due to difficulties in reaching an agreement and finally withdrawn in 2006,[40] and instead, priority was given to the implementation of the unitary patent.[41]

There is also continuous debate on the rationale of *sui generis* intellectual property regimes, especially given that they potentially undermine the strict demarcations of traditional intellectual property rights. Analyzing utility model regimes and their role in enhancing economic development and innovation, Suthersanen offers three rationales for utility model *sui generis* laws: (1) ameliorating the defects of the national

[38] Uma Suthersanen, 'Function, Art and Fashion: Do We Need the EU Design Law?' 88/2011 Queen Mary School of Law Legal Studies Research Paper <https://papers.ssrn.com/sol3/papers.cfm?abstract_id=1945142> accessed 2 November 2021.

[39] Mark D. Janis, 'Second Tier Patent Protection' (1999) 40 Harvard International Law Journal 151 <https://www.repository.law.indiana.edu/facpub/543/> accessed 3 November 2021.

[40] European Commission. Internal Market, Industry, Entrepreneurship and SMEs. Utility Models. <https://ec.europa.eu/growth/industry/strategy/intellectual-property/patent-protection-eu/utility-models_en> accessed 21 December 2021.

[41] European Commission. Internal Market, Industry, Entrepreneurship and SMEs. Unitary Patent. <https://ec.europa.eu/growth/industry/strategy/intellectual-property/patent-protection-eu/unitary-patent_en> accessed 21 December 2021.

patent system; (2) preventing free riding in copying and encouraging innovation, especially in relation to small and medium-sized enterprises; and (3) improving the legal environment in developing countries. The above justifications turned out to work for the Chinese, German, and South Korean economies. However, by way of Australian example, Suthersanen shows that, for countries where the national economy and industries have reached higher levels of technological capacity, utility model regimes might not be as useful, since the low innovative step increases low-value patents, thus creating uncertainty and making the benefits of the innovation patent system illusory, especially as compared to its costs. The conclusion that Suthersanen makes is that utility model *sui generis* rights can be useful and may enhance innovation, but only in certain developing countries and at specific stages of their development.[42]

Thus, the legal nature and the rationales of *sui generis* intellectual property rights become the object of constant battle in both scholarly and political circles. Introduction and implementation of *sui generis* rights into the legal framework of various jurisdictions provide an opportunity to study the practical experience of different countries with such a special form of legal protection of intellectual property. This book will further continue with examining how the EU and the U.S. have dealt with extending intellectual property legal protection to new subject matter via introduction of *sui generis* rights. For this purpose, this volume will look into the case studies of three categories of subject matter that are often considered as requiring *sui generis* intellectual property protection, namely, databases, designs, and plant varieties.

[42] Uma Suthersanen 'Utility models: do they really serve national innovation strategies?' in Josef Drexl and Anselm Kamperman Sanders (eds) The Innovation Society and Intellectual Property (Edward Elgar 2019) 2 <https://www.elgaronline.com/view/edcoll/9781789902341/9781789902341.00010.xml> accessed 12 January 2022.

Chapter 2
Sui Generis Intellectual Property Protection for Databases

Original databases are generally protected against piracy by intellectual property legal regimes, primarily copyright. Other available instruments of protection of databases include unfair competition[1] and contract law. However, unfair competition rules come into play only in case of competitive situations and do not provide an economic right with a clear scope.[2] As to contract law, it imposes high administrative burdens of negotiating terms with each user and provider of data. Besides, protection by contract does not prevent from unauthorized downstream uses, which can be resolved through encryption, although being expensive and cumbersome to implement.[3]

Another approach to legal protection of databases was taken by the northern European countries, namely, Denmark, Finland, Iceland, Norway, and Sweden, and is known as the "Nordic catalogue rule", which is a common name for a set of provisions in the Copyright Acts of these five countries. Although the "catalogue rule" appears in the Copyright Acts, its legal nature lies in the area of neighboring rights, related to copyright from the point of view of legislative technique by providing references to such copyright law provisions as rules for products of joint efforts,

---

[1] See, e.g., *International News Service v. Associated Press*, 248 U.S. 215 (1918), a famous U.S. Supreme Court case that developed the misappropriation doctrine, in particular "hot news" misappropriation, in the unfair competition law. Further, in *Feist*, the U.S. Supreme Court cited Nimmer on Copyright, noting that "protection for the fruits of such research … may, in certain circumstances, be available under a theory of unfair competition" (Nimmer § 3.04, p. 3–23 (footnote omitted)). See also Estelle Derclaye, 'Can and should misappropriation also protect databases? A comparative approach' in Paul Torremans (ed), *Copyright law: a handbook of contemporary research* (Edward Elgar 2007).

[2] U.S. Copyright Office. Report on Legal Protection for Databases, August 1997, 7 <https://www.copyright.gov/reports/db4.pdf> accessed 25 January 2022.

[3] Committee on Data. International Science Council. Anne Linn, 'History of Database Protection: Legal Issues of Concern to the Scientific Community' 3 March 2000 <https://www.codata.info/data_access/linn.html> accessed 25 January 2022.

I. Kazeeva, *Sui Generis Intellectual Property Protection*, Perspectives in Law, Business and Innovation, https://doi.org/10.1007/978-981-99-8897-6_2

products published anonymously, definitions of publication, etc.[4] At the same time, the "catalogue rule" may be observed as being of a competition law character, aiming to protect enterprises' investments in producing compilations. The catalogue rule covered "catalogues, tables, and similar compilations in which a large number of particulars have been summarized",[5] thus demanding no creativeness manifested in individuality or originality. The protection was granted against reproduction and lasted ten years, starting at the end of the year of publication.[6]

Collections as protectable subject matter are mentioned in international agreements. Under Article 2(5) of the Berne Convention, "collections of literary or artistic works such as encyclopedias and anthologies which, by reason of the selection and arrangement of their contents, constitute intellectual creations shall be protected as such, without prejudice to the copyright in each of the works forming part of such collections". Compilations were introduced into the Berne Convention under the 1908 Berlin Act[7] as "collections of different works" (Article 2(2)). The present wording as a separate paragraph was introduced under the 1948 Brussels Act,[8] which became Article 2(5) at the Stockholm Conference in 1967.[9]

The Convention lays down an important condition: the collection, by reason of selection or[10] arrangement, must be an intellectual creation, i.e., the maker must bring an element of creativity, "merely listing the works or extracts without offering any personal contribution is not enough".[11] "Selection" covers the choice of works for the collection and should be broad enough to include the activity of editing, whereas "arrangement" involves deciding how to present the collection.[12] Although there remains disagreement as to whether the Berne Convention imposes an obligation on the member states to protect non-copyright subject matter, most commentators have concluded that Article 2(5) covers any subject matter (both copyright

---

[4] Gunnar Karnell, 'The Nordic Catalogue Rule' in E.J. Dommering & P.B. Hugenholtz (eds.), *Protecting Works of Fact* (Kluwer Law and Taxation Publishers 1991).

[5] Section 49 of the 1960 Act on Copyright in Literary and Artistic Works of Sweden. The current version of Section 49 includes compilations which are the result of a significant investment and grants protection for fifteen years. See WIPO, Act on Copyright in Literary and Artistic Works (Swedish Statute Book, SFS, 1960:729, as last amended by SFS 2020:540) <https://wipolex-res.wipo.int/edocs/lexdocs/laws/en/se/se225en.html> accessed 8 July 2022.

[6] Gunnar Karnell, 'The Nordic Catalogue Rule' (n 4).

[7] WIPO. Acte de Berlin (1908) <https://wipolex.wipo.int/en/text/278699> accessed 4 July 2022.

[8] WIPO. Brussles Act (1948) <https://wipolex.wipo.int/en/text/278722> accessed 4 July 2022.

[9] WIPO. Stockholm Act (1967) <https://wipolex-res.wipo.int/edocs/lexdocs/treaties/en/berne/trt_berne_003en.pdf> accessed 4 July 2022.

[10] The French text of Article 2(5) of the Berne Convention says: "par le choix ou la disposition des matières". Under Article 37(1)(c) of the Convention, the French text shall prevail in case of differences in interpretation.

[11] WIPO. Guide to the Berne Convention for the Protection of Literary and Artistic Works (Paris Act, 1971) <https://www.wipo.int/edocs/pubdocs/en/copyright/615/wipo_pub_615.pdf> accessed 5 July 2022.

[12] Sam Ricketson and Jane Ginsburg, 'International Copyright and Neighboring Rights. The Berne Convention and Beyond' (Oxford University Press, 2022) par. 8.88.

and non-copyright) resulting from "intellectual", i.e., non-mechanical, selection or arrangement of the contents.[13]

This approach is confirmed by the TRIPS Agreement saying that protection of compilations of data or material shall be without prejudice to any copyright subsisting in the data or material itself (Article 10(2)). The TRIPS Agreement requires the same standard of originality as the Berne Convention, but has a broader scope of application, covering all "compilations of data or other material, whether in machine readable or other form", whereas the Berne Convention applies only to literary and artistic works.

Article 5 of the WIPO Copyright Treaty,[14] providing protection to authors in the digital environment, further simplified this wording by covering "compilations of data or other material, in any form".

Still, a large number of databases could not meet the originality requirement, despite the significant investment made to produce them. This fact prompted the WIPO member states to present a Basic Proposal for the Substantive Provisions of the Treaty on Intellectual Property in Respect of Databases to be considered by the Diplomatic Conference[15] in 1996. The treaty, based on the proposals of the EU and the U.S., was supposed to grant protection to "all databases that represent a substantial investment".[16] However, the attempt to create an international *sui generis* system of protection of databases was met with strong opposition, and the Proposal was not adopted.

The opponents of *sui generis* protection of databases include academic societies, libraries, telecommunication companies, Internet service providers. The critics of the *sui generis* protection model claim that such a legal regime would result in excluding people from access to information, that would impede scientific research, hinder creativity and discussion.[17] Nevertheless, in the same year when the proposal for a *sui generis* system of protection of databases was declined at WIPO, a Directive introducing a similar regime was adopted in the EU.

2.1 Legal Protection of Databases in the EU

The need for a *sui generis* database right in the EU originated, on the one hand, from inadequacy of copyright in protecting database producers and, on the other hand, from lack of harmonization of copyright law in different Member States.

[13] Daniel J. Gervais, 'The Protection of Databases'(2007) 82 Chicago-Kent Law Review 1109.

[14] WIPO Copyright Treaty <https://wipolex.wipo.int/en/text/295157> accessed 5 July 2022.

[15] WIPO. Diplomatic conference on certain copyright and neighboring rights questions. Geneva, December 2 to 20, 1996. Basic Proposal for the Substantive Provisions of the Treaty on Intellectual Property in Respect of Databases to be considered by the Diplomatic Conference <https://www.wipo.int/edocs/mdocs/diplconf/en/crnr_dc/crnr_dc_6.pdf> accessed 6 July 2022.

[16] Ibid, notes on Article 1, section 1.01.

[17] Taiwo A. Oriola, 'Electronic Database Protection and the Limits of Copyright: What Options for Developing Countries' (2004) 7 Journal of World Intellectual Property 201, 226–227.

In its Green Paper on Copyright and the Challenge of Technology published in 1988,[18] the Commission of the European Communities noted that "information broking", i.e., buying and selling of databases containing factual information, is a growing industry and therefore requires a clear legal framework. It was suggested to consider whether "the investment which a compilation of data may represent, and which may not attract copyright protection, necessitates some protection against unauthorized reproduction".[19] Still, this suggestion was not upheld at a hearing held in April 1990, where a large majority of participants rejected the *sui generis* approach.[20]

However, the court decisions that followed both in the EU and the U.S. changed the overall skepticism about a *sui generis* system. In 1991, the Dutch Supreme Court set the boundaries of applicability of copyright protection for databases in the case *Van Dale v. Romme*.[21] Romme copied headwords from the Van Dale dictionary, one of the most authoritative dictionaries of the Dutch language, onto computer disks and created a database, which, with a searching algorithm, sped up the solving of crossword puzzles. Reversing the decision of the Amsterdam Court of Appeals on copyright protection of the Van Dale's compilation of headwords, the Supreme Court stated that "in order for a product to be considered as a work of literature, science or art ..., it is required that it has its own, original character and bears the personal imprint of the maker. A collection of words that are part of the Dutch language does not automatically meet this requirement. ...That would only be different if the collection were the result of a selection that expresses the maker's personal vision".[22] In *Endstra v. Nieuw Amsterdam*,[23] the Dutch Supreme Court noted that the personal imprint of the maker means that "there must be a form which is the result of creative human work and thus of creative choices, and therefore is a product of a human mind. Outside this falls in any case a form which is so banal or trivial, that no creative work of any kind can be identified behind it".[24]

In that same year, another famous case, *Feist Publications, Inc. v. Rural Telephone Service Co., Inc.*,[25] was decided by the U.S. Supreme Court denying protection to

---

[18] Publications Office of the European Union. Green Paper on Copyright and The Challenge Of Technology—Copyright Issues Requiring Immediate Action. Communication from The Commission <https://op.europa.eu/en/publication-detail/-/publication/a3392acf-2b75-11e7-9412-01aa75ed71a1/language-en/format-PDF/source-search> accessed 8 July 2022.

[19] Ibid, para 6.4.7.

[20] Publications Office of the European Union. Follow-Up To The Green Paper—Working Programme Of The Commission In The Field Of Copyright And Neighboring Rights <https://op.europa.eu/en/publication-detail/-/publication/c988b07e-064a-44df-a835-26f0019bc7b6> accessed 9 July 2022.

[21] *Van Dale Lexicografie B.V. v. Rudolf Jan Romme* Supreme Court of the Netherlands NJ 1991/608 (1991).

[22] Para 3.4.

[23] *Endstra v. Uitgerverij Nieuw Amsterdam* Supreme Court of the Netherlands C07/131HR (2008).

[24] Para 4.5.1.

[25] *Feist Publications, Inc. v. Rural Telephone Service Co., Inc.* U.S. Supreme Court 111 S.Ct. 1282 (1991).

databases produced by sweat of the brow. It is widely acknowledged that both the *Van Dale v. Romme* and *Feist* decisions partly triggered the introduction of *sui generis* intellectual property protection for databases in the EU.[26]

In 1992, the European Commission presented a Proposal for a Council Directive on the Legal Protection of Databases.[27] In the Explanatory Memorandum, accompanying the Proposal, the Commission noted that in none of the legislation of the Member States are databases explicitly protected (Section 2.2.3 of Part One). Besides, the Commission highlighted significant differences in the copyright protection granted by Member States, particularly the difference in the standard of originality, term of protection, ability of a user of a database of downloading (reproduction) of the database, and exceptions for educational or private use (Sections 2.2.5–2.2.7). Such differences in the legal protection of databases, especially between common law and *droit d'auteur* Member States, have negative effects on the free movement of database products. The Commission concluded that "there is clearly a need to establish at least a basic harmonized framework" of the legal protection of databases, otherwise "there is a risk that Member States may legislate expressly in widely differing ways, or that Community databases fall victim to misappropriation because of an absence of enforceable protection" (Section 2.2.11).

In Section 3.2 "Relationship between protection of the database and its contents" of the Explanatory Memorandum, the Commission observed that "in some instances neither the selection nor the arrangement criteria will afford sufficient room for individual choices to be made by the author", e.g., in case of arrangement in alphabetical order. In these circumstances, copyright protection should subsist neither in the first, nor in the subsequent collections. However, even the mere accumulation of facts involves significant "commercial activity, time, labour and organizational skills".

As to the choice of the appropriate legal regime for protection of databases (Section 5 of the Explanatory Memorandum), the Commission noted that neither copyright protection, nor a *sui generis* regime alone may be an adequate solution to the problems raised by the protection of databases. It therefore proposed a two-tier approach that would include copyright protection, applied in conformity with the Berne Convention, and a special *sui generis* right, "which is derived from regimes such as unfair competition law or the law repressing parasitic behaviour".

In 1993, the European Parliament approved the Proposal, subject to a large number of amendments. After a series of discussions and revisions, the Directive on the legal protection of databases[28] ("Database Directive") was finally enacted on 11 March 1996.[29]

---

[26] Paul Goldstein and Bernt Hugenholtz, *International Copyright* (Oxford University Press Second edition 2010) 240.

[27] Proposal for a Council Directive on the Legal Protection of Databases, COM (92)24 final [1992] OJ 1992 C156/4.

[28] Directive 96/9/EC of 11 March 1996 on the legal protection of databases [1996] OJ L 77/20.

[29] Procedure 1992/0393/COD. COM (1992) 24: Proposal for a Council Directive on the legal protection of databases <https://eur-lex.europa.eu/procedure/EN/1992_393> accessed 14 July 2022.

The Database Directive opens with defining databases that are to be granted protection. "Database" means a collection of independent works, data, or other materials arranged in a systematic or methodical way and individually accessible by electronic or other means (Article 1). There are several conditions to be met in order for a collection to qualify as a database under the Database Directive. First, it should be "a collection of works, data or other materials", thus covering a wide range of materials, "such as texts, sound, images, numbers, facts, and data". Second, the elements comprising a database should be independent, systematically or methodically arranged, and it should be possible to access them individually. Thus, recordings or an audiovisual, cinematographic, literary or musical works as such cannot be treated as collections of sounds, images, etc. and do not fall within the scope of the Database Directive (Recital 17). At the same time, it is not necessary for those materials to have been physically stored in an organized manner (Recital 21). The Database Directive may apply to the materials necessary for the operation or consultation of certain databases, such as thesaurus and indexation systems (Recital 20), however computer programs used in the making or operation of databases are explicitly excluded from the scope of the Database Directive (Article 1).

The Database Directive provides two-tier protection stipulated in Chapter II "Copyright" and Chapter III "*Sui Generis* Right". Copyright protection is granted to databases which, by reason of the selection or arrangement of their contents, constitute the author's own intellectual creation (Article 3). This provision is reminiscent to Article 10(2) of the TRIPS Agreement, requiring the same standard of originality. The Database Directive further lists exclusive rights of the author of a database to be protected by copyright: right to reproduction, translation, any alteration, distribution, communication to the public (Article 5) and allows for exceptions that are traditionally found in copyright laws of the Member States (normal use by a lawful user, reproduction for private purposes of a non-electronic database,[30] use for the purpose of teaching or scientific research, public security, administrative or judicial procedure) (Article 6).

However, according to Hugenholtz, copyright in databases provides "thin" protection, as copying part of a database, without appropriating "selection or arrangement" of the data, does not amount to copyright infringement. Therefore, the most important part of the Database Directive is Chapter III, providing for legal protection via *sui generis* regime.[31]

The Directive distinguishes databases protected by copyright, which must satisfy the originality threshold, from databases which do not meet that threshold and which

[30] Thus, reproduction for private purposes of electronic databases is not allowed. According to Hugenholtz, the European legislature has apparently been convinced by the rightholders' lobbying that "digital is different". See P. Bernt Hugenholtz, 'Implementing the European Database Directive' in Jan J. C. Kabel and Gerard J. H. M. Mom (eds.), *Intellectual Property and Information Law, Essays in Honour of Herman Cohen Jehoram* (The Hague/London/Boston: Kluwer Law International 1998).

[31] P. Bernt Hugenholtz, 'Implementing the European Database Directive' in Jan J. C. Kabel and Gerard J. H. M. Mom (eds.), *Intellectual Property and Information Law, Essays in Honour of Herman Cohen Jehoram* (The Hague/London/Boston: Kluwer Law International 1998).

are entitled to *sui generis* right to prevent extraction or reutilization of a substantial part of their contents.[32] "Extraction" means permanent or temporary transfer of all or a substantial part of the contents of a database to another medium, while "reutilization" is making available to the public the contents of a database by the distribution of copies, renting, online, etc. Besides, the first sale doctrine shall apply in case of a first sale of a copy of a database by, or with the consent of, the rightholder (Article 7 of the Database Directive).

Unlike copyright, which protects only the original structure of the database (the selection or arrangement of contents), the *sui generis* right protects the contents themselves, provided that there has been a substantial investment in obtaining, verification, or presentation of the contents. "Obtaining" refers to seeking material and collecting it in a database, "verification" means checking, correcting, and updating the data, and "presentation" involves communication of the complied data.[33]The investment can be qualitative or quantitative, and may consist in the deployment of financial resources and/or the expending of time, effort and energy (Recital 40 of the Database Directive). Thus, the *sui generis* right protects the "sweat of the brow" of the database producer, i.e., the skill, energy, and money invested in the database.[34] The right is granted to the maker of the database, i.e., the person who takes the initiative and the risk of investing (Recital 41).

The Directive offers little guidance as to what investment shall amount to substantial. However, Recital 19 specifically points out that compilation of recordings of musical performances on a CD does not come within the scope of the Database Directive, "both because, as a compilation, it does not meet the conditions for copyright protection and because it does not represent a substantial enough investment to be eligible under the *sui generis* right". Nor does the Database Directive defines what amounts to a "substantial part" of the contents of the database.

As noted above, the *sui generis* right was initially viewed as "derived from regimes such as unfair competition law or the law repressing parasitic behaviour" (Section 5.3.6 of the Explanatory Memorandum). Indeed, instead of the term "*sui generis* right" used in the final version of the Database Directive, the initial 1992 Proposal contained the term "right to prevent unfair extraction", meaning the right of the maker of a database to prevent acts of extraction and re-utilization of material from that database for commercial purposes (Article 1 of the Proposal).

However, in the enacted version of the Database Directive, the right has moved away from competition law. Gaster observes that, unlike the law of unfair competition, the database *sui generis* right also covers acts committed by users in non-competitive situations, creates exclusive rights *a priori* (instead of only sanctioning behavior *a posteriori*), and grants a term of protection, therefore being similar in

---

[32] Graham Greenleaf and David Lindsay, 'Public Rights: Copyright's Public Domains' (Cambridge University Press 2018) 192.

[33] Paul Goldstein and P. Bernt Hugenholtz, *International Copyright* (n 26).

[34] P. Bernt Hugenholtz, 'Implementing the European Database Directive' (n 30).

nature to intellectual property rights.[35] Recital 42 explicitly mentions that the right relates not only to the manufacture of a parasitical competing product but also to any user who, through his acts, causes significant detriment to the investment. Besides, Article 7(3) of the Database Directive allows the *sui generis* right to be transferred, assigned or granted under contractual license, which makes it a "full-fledged property right".[36]

According to Hugenholtz, the *sui generis* database right is akin to the neighboring rights of phonogram and film producers. Both neighboring rights and the EU database right were grounded in the financial investments involved by the producers of phonograms, broadcasters, and creators of databases (except for the neighboring right of performers, which has a different rationale, similar to the *raison d'être* of author's rights). However, the requirement of substantial investment in databases makes the EU database right more justified as opposed to the phonographic right, broadcaster's right and EU film producer's right with no technological investment threshold.[37] Moreover, Hugenholtz notes, the absence of a threshold test results in overprotection in cases where the recording, broadcasting, or filming require little to no investment, which is very often the case nowadays, as opposed to the mid-twentieth century, when these rights (except for the film producers' rights) were secured in the Rome Convention.[38]

The *sui generis* database right is also viewed as akin to publisher's right. Publishers are neither authors nor related rights owners, but they organize the supply of information via their creative role in designing the flow of information and their financial investments. In 2000, Clark noted that the *sui generis* right in the Database Directive is as near as publishers were ever likely to get to a publisher's right.[39] In 2019, the neighboring right for press publishers was introduced in the Digital Single Market Directive.[40] Hugenholtz observes that the new neighboring right seems to have its justification in the investment in content aggregation, quite similar to the *sui generis* database right.[41] However, same as the previous neighboring rights, the publisher's right lacks a threshold test, which, on the one hand, will lead to overprotection and

[35] Jens L. Gaster, 'The New EU Directive concerning the Legal Protection of Databases' (1996) 20 Fordham Int.L.J. 1129.

[36] P. Bernt Hugenholtz, 'Implementing the European Database Directive' (n 30).

[37] P. Bernt Hugenholtz, 'Neighboring Rights are Obsolete' 2019 <https://link.springer.com/content/pdf/10.1007/s40319-019-00864-3.pdf> accessed 27 November 2021.

[38] International Convention for the Protection of Performers, Producers of Phonograms and Broadcasting Organisations. Rome, 26 October 1961 <https://treaties.un.org/pages/ViewDetails.aspx?src=TREATY&mtdsg_no=XIV-3&chapter=14&clang=_en> accessed 20 February 2023.

[39] Charles Clark, 'Net Law: A Cyberspace Agenda for Publishers' (2000) 3 The Journal of World Intellectual Property 97,110 <https://ur.booksc.eu/book/10123267/8c60f9> accessed 24 January 2022.

[40] Directive (EU) 2019/790 of the European Parliament and of the Council of 17 April 2019 on copyright and related rights in the Digital Single Market and amending Directives 96/9/EC and 2001/29/EC [2019] OJ L130/92.

[41] P. Bernt Hugenholtz, 'Neighboring Rights are Obsolete' (n 37).

legal uncertainty and, on the other hand, again demonstrates that the EU database right appears to be more justified.

Because of this similarity between *sui generis* right and neighboring rights, the database *sui generis* right has been transposed as a special neighboring right in Germany, France, Spain, Portugal, and Italy. In Belgium and Netherlands, the right has been transposed by a special act, illustrating its *sui generis* status.[42]

The Database Directive provides for standard exceptions to the *sui generis* right, such as extraction for private purposes, teaching and scientific research, public security, administrative or judicial procedures (Article 9). The term of protection is fifteen years from the date of completion of the database, starting from the first of January of the year following creation of the database. In case of a substantial change that is considered a substantial new investment, a new term of protection will start for the resulting database (Article 10). This means that a regularly updated database is granted permanent protection.[43]

Unlike copyright protection that, under the Berne Convention, is also provided to nationals and residents of third countries, the *sui generis* database right is granted only to nationals of Member States and companies having their registered office and principal place of business within the Community (Article 11). However, reciprocity agreements may be concluded.[44]

Since the enactment of the Database Directive, the European Commission has published two evaluation reports in 2005 and 2018.[45] In the first evaluation report, the Commission observed that the economic impact of the database *sui generis* right is unproven and the empirical evidence casts doubts on its necessity for a thriving database industry. However, it was also noted that most respondents in the online survey had found that the *sui generis* database right "has brought about legal certainty, reduced the costs associated with the protection of databases, created more business opportunities, and facilitated the marketing of databases" (Section 1.4). Therefore, most European publishers and database producers preferred to retain the *sui generis* protection. Although its impact in stimulating the production of databases is limited, the Database Directive does not impose significant administrative or regulatory burdens. Thus, the Commission concludes that one of the policy options is leaving the Database Directive unchanged (Section 1.5).

In 2004, the ECJ delivered judgements on four cases concerning the database *sui generis* right.[46] According to the Commission, these ECJ judgements have pointed

---

[42] Paul Goldstein and P. Bernt Hugenholtz, *International Copyright* (n 26) 239–240.

[43] P. Bernt Hugenholtz, 'Implementing the European Database Directive' (n 30).

[44] Jens L. Gaster, 'The New EU Directive concerning the Legal Protection of Databases' (n 35) 1148.

[45] European Commission. Staff working document and executive summary on the evaluation of the Directive 96/9/EC on the legal protection of databases <https://digital-strategy.ec.europa.eu/en/library/staff-working-document-and-executive-summary-evaluation-directive-969ec-legal-protection-databases> accessed 18 July 2022.

[46] Case C-46/02 *Fixtures Marketing Ltd v. Oy Veikkaus Ab* [2004] ECR I-10365; case C-203/02 *The British Horseracing Board Ltd and Others v. William Hill Organisation Ltd* [2004] ECR I-10415; case C-338/02 *Fixtures Marketing Limited v. AB Svenska Spel* [2004] ECR I-10497; case C-444/02

to serious difficulties raised by applying "untested and ambiguous legal concepts" (Section 4.1.4 of the evaluation report). Particularly, in *The British Horseracing Board Ltd and Others v. William Hill Organisation Ltd*, the ECJ ruled that "obtaining" of the contents of the database means seeking out existing independent materials rather than creation of such materials. Thus, the Court concluded, "the resources used to draw up a list of horses in a race and to carry out checks in that connection do not represent investment in the obtaining and verification of the contents of the database" and are therefore not subject to protection under the *sui generis* right. Therefore, databases which are the by-products of the main activities of an economic undertaking are not protected by the *sui generis* right. It is further assumed that the *sui generis* right does not apply broadly to the data economy, only covering databases that contain data obtained from external sources.

In the second evaluation report, although admitting that the *sui generis* right continues to have no proven impact on stimulating the production of databases in the EU or raising competitiveness of the EU databases, the Commission noted a number of positive effects of the Database Directive. First, the Directive has effectively harmonized the national laws of the Members States on protection of databases. Second, although both benefits and costs of the *sui generis* right are moderate, the benefits are higher. Particularly, both database makers and users benefit from the legal clarity provided by the Database Directive. Thirdly, the Database Directive is "very relevant as it restricts regulatory fragmentation that could be detrimental to the Digital Single Market". Therefore, the Commission concludes, there is no need, at this stage, for reforming the *sui generis* right, and keeping the *status quo* seems to be a good option.

Thus, the introduction of the database *sui generis* right in the EU has had a number of significant positive effects, one of them being harmonization of the laws regulating database legal protection in the Member States. Although the *sui generis* right has not shown a proven economic effect, the involved stakeholders clearly benefit from this novel right since it provides legal clarity.

However, the EU *sui generis* database right has also come under strong criticism. In 2002, the Standing Committee on Copyright and Related Rights of the WIPO published a study on the protection of unoriginal databases. In the study, four arguments in favor of *sui generis* database protection (including protection of investments, advantageous position of European companies, motivation for creation of databases in developing countries) are followed by eleven arguments against such protection. These arguments include broad scope and potentially perpetual term of protection, increase of the cost of research, hampering software development, concentration of market power in the Internet, etc.[47]

Fixtures Marketing Ltd v. Organismos prognostikon agonon podosfairou AE (OPAP) [2004] ECR I-10549.

[47] WIPO. Standing Committee on Copyright and Related Rights. Seventh Session, Geneva, May 13–17, 2002. Study on the Protection of Unoriginal Databases <https://www.wipo.int/edocs/mdocs/copyright/en/sccr_7/sccr_7_3.pdf> accessed 20 December 2022.

The *sui generis* database right may also hinder the development of AI and machine learning. In particular, Kop claims that the EU should revise the Database Directive in order to prevent machine generated data from qualifying for *sui generis* database protection.[48]

The need to limit the application of the *sui generis* database right has been at least partially recognized by the EU, which is demonstrated by the explicit exclusions from the *sui generis* regime in the recent legal acts. The Data Act,[49] which ensures that a wider range of stakeholders gain control over their data and more data is available for innovative use, explicitly states that the *sui generis* database right shall not apply to databases containing data obtained from, or generated by, a connected product or related service (Article 43). Thus, the Data Act aims to ensure that the *sui generis* right will not interfere with rights for businesses and consumers to access, use, and share data. Similarly, the Data Governance Act,[50] being, along with the Data Act, the key pillar of the European strategy for data,[51] excludes the exercise of the database *sui generis* right by public sector bodies in order to prevent or restrict the re-use of data (Article 5(7)), which is similar to the exclusion provided for in Article 1(6) of the Open Data Directive.[52] Summarizing these recent legislative exclusions from the applicability of the *sui generis* database right, Keller writes that every time the EU attempts to create a modern regulatory framework for the data economy, the database *sui generis* right loses out, thus turning into a "right that shall not be exercised".[53] This raises the question as to how much scope of application of the *sui generis* database right remains, taking into account the CJEU case law and the exclusions provided for in the Data Act, Data Governance Act, and the Open Data Directive.

At the same time, one of the main goals initially set by the Database Directive was to close the gap in production of databases between the EU and the U.S. This goal has not been achieved, with the U.S. remaining the leader in production of databases, even without a special intellectual property right for their protection.

---

[48] Mauritz Kop, 'The Right to Process Data for Machine Learning Purposes in the EU' (2021) 34 Harvard Journal of Law & Technology <https://jolt.law.harvard.edu/digest/the-right-to-process-data-for-machine-learning-purposes-in-the-eu> accessed 20 December 2022.

[49] Regulation (EU) 2023/2854 of the European Parliament and of the Council of 13 December 2023 on harmonised rules on fair access to and use of data and amending Regulation (EU) 2017/2394 and Directive (EU) 2020/1828 (Data Act) [2023] OJ L2023/2854.

[50] Regulation (EU) 2022/868 of the European Parliament and of the Council of 30 May 2022 on European data governance and amending Regulation (EU) 2018/1724 (Data Governance Act) [2022] OJ L 152/1.

[51] Communication from the Commission to the European Parliament the Council, the European Economic and Social Committee and the Committee of the Regions. A European strategy for data. COM/2020/66 final.

[52] Directive (EU) 2019/1024 of the European Parliament and of the Council of 20 June 2019 on open data and the re-use of public sector information [2019] OJ L172/56.

[53] Paul Keller, 'A vanishing right? The Sui Generis Database Right and the proposed Data Act' Kluwer Copyright Blog, 4 March 2022 <http://copyrightblog.kluweriplaw.com/2022/03/04/a-vanishing-right-the-sui-generis-database-right-and-the-proposed-data-act/> accessed 31 July 2022.

2.2 Legal Protection of Databases in the U.S.

According to the Gale Directory of Databases, the number of databases published in the EU in 2013 amounts to 4,864, whereas in the U.S. this figure was 14,604, which amounts to 21 and 67% of the world production of databases, respectively.[54] Thus, the U.S. remains the leader in the production of databases, doing without a special legal regime for their legal protection.

In the terminology of copyright law, database represents a compilation. The term "compilation" was introduced in the U.S. copyright law by the Copyright Act of 1976[55] and is defined as "a work formed by the collection and assembling of preexisting materials or of data that are selected, coordinated, or arranged in such a way that the resulting work as a whole constitutes an original work of authorship".[56] In the U.S., compilations have been protected as books since the eighteenth century under the Copyright Act of 1790.[57] In particular, protection was granted to a "map, chart, or book" for 14 years from recordation of the printed title of the work in the register book. Interestingly, the word "book" had a broad meaning extending to a diverse array of compilations of information.[58]

Since the nineteenth century, the courts applied two rationales for granting copyright protection to compilations: the "sweat of the brow" doctrine, focused on the effort and investment of the compiler, and the originality doctrine, focused on compiler's creativity in the selection and arrangement of materials.

This practice changed with the Supreme Court decision in *Feist Publications v. Rural Telephone Service Co.* The plaintiff, Rural Telephone Service Company, provided telephone services to a number of communities in Kansas and was under a statutory obligation to issue annual telephone directories. Feist Publications, a publishing company, used the data from the directories prepared by Rural to prepare its own phone directories covering a larger area after Rural had refused to license the data to Feist. Rural filed a claim for copyright infringement, which was upheld by the District Court and the Court of Appeals. However, the Supreme Court reversed the decision, holding that "copyright protects only those constituent elements of a work that possess more than a *de minimis* quantum of creativity", while "Rural's white pages, limited to basic subscriber information and arranged alphabetically, fall short of the mark". The Court particularly stressed that the decision should be construed not as demeaning Rural's efforts in compiling the directory, but as making clear that copyright rewards originality, not effort. Thus, the Supreme Court pronounced

[54] See Commission Staff Working Document "Evaluation of Directive 96/9/EC on the legal protection of databases" WD(2018) 147 final <https://digital-strategy.ec.europa.eu/en/library/staff-working-document-and-executive-summary-evaluation-directive-969ec-legal-protection-databases> accessed 20 July 2022.

[55] 90 Stat. 2541.

[56] 17 U.S.C. § 101.

[57] Copyright Act of 31 May 1790, ch. 15, 1 Stat. 124.

[58] William F. Patry, 'Copyright Law and Practice' (Bureau of National Affairs 1994) <https://digital-law-online.info/patry/patry5.html#_ftnref90> accessed 31 January 2022.

creative originality as the main criterion of copyrightability, which "sounded the death knell for the sweat of the brow doctrine".[59]

At the same time, the Court also stated that the vast majority of works meet the originality test quite easily, as they possess some creative spark, no matter how crude, humble, or obvious it might be. According to section 312.2 "Compilations and Collective Works" of the Compendium of U.S. Copyright Office Practices, "in determining whether a compilation satisfies the originality requirement, the registration specialist should focus on the manner in which the materials or data have been selected, coordinated, and arranged and the principal focus should be on whether the selection, coordination, and arrangement are sufficiently original to merit protection".[60]

Indeed, the subsequent cases have proven that the majority of databases still met the originality requirement, despite the *Feist* decision. In *Key Publications, Inc. v. Chinatown Today Publishing Enterprises Inc.*,[61] the Court applied the originality test from the Feist decision to confirm copyrightability of a yellow pages business directory for the New York Chinese American community. In *Kregos v. Associated Press*,[62] the Court stated that the plaintiff's baseball pitching form comprised of data rating pitcher's performance is entitled to copyright protection, since the plaintiff's selection of statistics for the pitching form displayed sufficient creativity to satisfy the originality requirement. In *CCC Information Services v. Maclean Hunter Market Reports, Inc.*,[63] the Court held that the originality standard was satisfied in Maclean's compilation of used-car valuations, stating that the valuations in the Red Book represented predictions by the editors of future prices and were based on professional judgment and expertise. The Court, again, stressed that the thrust of the Supreme Court's ruling in Feist was not to erect a high barrier of originality requirement, but rather to specify that some originality is essential to protection of authorship.

Despite the fact that *Feist* did not significantly affect the court practice and majority of databases could still meet the minimum originality standard, the Supreme Court decision triggered a number of legislative initiatives for introducing a special regime of legal protection of databases. However, none of those bills have become law. Besides providing protection for the U.S. database producers, one of the rationales was to secure protection of the U.S. databases in the EU under the Database Directive, which granted *sui generis* protection to databases from other jurisdictions only if such jurisdictions offered comparable protection (Recital 56 of the EU Database Directive).

---

[59] U.S. Copyright Office. Report on Legal Protection for Databases, August 1997, 7 <https://www.copyright.gov/reports/db4.pdf> accessed 25 January 2022.

[60] U.S. Copyright Office, Compendium of U.S. Copyright Office Practices § 101 (3d ed. 2021) <https://www.copyright.gov/comp3/> accessed 3 February 2022.

[61] 945 F.2d 509 (2d Cir. 1991).

[62] 937 F.2d 700 (2d Cir. 1991).

[63] 44 F.3d 61 (2d Cir. 1994).

The first U.S. database protection bill H.R. 3531 was introduced in the House of Representatives in 1996. The proposed Database Investment and Intellectual Property Antipiracy Act was modeled after the EU Database Directive and specified that a database is subject to protection "if it is the result of a substantial investment of human, technical, financial, or other resources in the collection, assembly, verification, organization, or presentation of the database contents and the database is used or reused in commerce".[64] The bill proposed a term of protection of 25 years (as opposed to fifteen years under the EU Database Directive) and potential criminal penalties, which included imprisonment up to 10 years, without providing for fair use exceptions. These provisions caused strong opposition in the library and scientific communities, and no further action was taken on the bill.[65]

Another bill, Collections of Information Antipiracy Act (H.R. 2652),[66] was introduced in the House of Representatives in 1997. The bill was subsequently folded into a copyright bill, and since a compromise on the database provisions could not be reached, they were removed whereas the copyright provisions became law.[67]

In 1999, two further bills were introduced to prevent parasitic copying of databases—the Collections of Information Antipiracy Act (H.R. 354)[68] and the Consumer and Investor Access to Information Act (H.R. 1858).[69] The first bill proposed to amend the Federal Copyright Act to make liable any persons who make available to others, or who extract, or use in commerce, a substantial part of a collection of information gathered or maintained by another person through the investment of substantial resources. The second bill proscribed the sale or distribution to the public of any database that (1) is a duplicate of another database, and (2) is sold or distributed in commerce in competition with that other database. Thus, H.R. 354 was aimed at providing protection to the producers of databases, whereas H.R. 1858 was oriented towards database users, as it allowed all uses of databases, provided such use did not compete in commerce with the original database. H.R. 354, McManis argued, would create a *sui generis* right, analogous to the right under the Database Directive, whereas H.R. 1858 would do little more than federally codify the common law tort of "hot news" misappropriation.[70] However, both of these bills lapsed.

---

[64] H.R.3531—Database Investment and Intellectual Property Antipiracy Act of 1996. 104th Congress (1995–1996) <https://www.congress.gov/bill/104th-congress/house-bill/3531?r=518&s=1> accessed 15 February 2022.

[65] Committee on Data. International Science Council. Anne Linn, 'History of Database Protection: Legal Issues of Concern to the Scientific Community' 3 March 2000 <https://www.codata.info/data_access/linn.html> accessed 25 January 2022.

[66] H.R.2652—Collections of Information Antipiracy Act. 105th Congress (1997–1998) <https://www.congress.gov/bill/105th-congress/house-bill/2652/text> accessed 21 October 2022.

[67] Ibid.

[68] H.R.354—Collections of Information Antipiracy Act. 106th Congress (1999–2000) <https://www.congress.gov/bill/106th-congress/house-bill/354> accessed 21 July 2022.

[69] H.R.1858—Consumer and Investor Access to Information Act of 1999. 106th Congress (1999–2000) <https://www.congress.gov/bill/106th-congress/house-bill/1858> accessed 21 July 2022.

[70] Charles R. McManis, 'Database Protection in the Digital Information Age' (2001) 7 Roger Williams University Law Review 7.

The latest attempt to introduce database legal protection was the Database and Collections of Information Misappropriation Act (H.R. 3261)[71] and a bill, introduced as its counterpart, Consumer Access to Information Act (H.R. 3872).[72] The former bill makes civilly liable any person who makes available in commerce to others a substantial part of the information of a database without authorization of the database producer. Whereas the latter prohibited the misappropriation of a database by classifying such misappropriation as an unfair method of competition under the Federal Trade Commission Act. In the end, both bills lapsed at the end of the 108th session of Congress.

As McManis observes, the emergence of such competing bills demonstrates that the reciprocity provision in the EU Database Directive was foisting a new regime of intellectual property protection on the U.S., which is precisely the same tactic as the U.S. used in 1984, inducing other states to create a *sui generis* right for semiconductor chips.[73]

Sui generis protection for databases also did not find support among many U.S. scholars. Davison, for example, discusses the difficulties that emerged in the application of the database *sui generis* right that resulted in cases referred to the ECJ, as well as the fact that the EU Database Directive has not achieved its intended result and, according to the 2005 evaluation report, has not had a positive impact on the production of databases in the EU. He continues that the blindingly obvious lesson that one should learn from the EU's experience with the Database Directive is that "the U.S. does not need *sui generis* database protection. Nor does anyone else. Any proposal for it should go in the bin. Not even the recycling bin because the last thing you need is the proposal coming back. Put it in the trash and empty the trash".[74]

Leaffer considers that the cost of a *sui generis* database law outweighs its benefits.[75] Referring to the Database Directive, he writes that "once a law is on the books—even a bad one—it is difficult to get rid of it" and that for Europe "it seems too late to go back in time". As to the legal protection of databases in the U.S., Leaffer stresses that "database owners of all varieties are well taken care of", and their ability to protect databases "is robust and flourishing, even without a specialized *sui generis* protection".

---

[71] H.R. 3261—Database and Collections of Information Misappropriation Act. 108th Congress (2003–2004) <https://www.congress.gov/bill/108th-congress/house-bill/3261?q=H.R.+3261+%28108%29> accessed 20 July 2022.

[72] H.R.3872—Consumer Access to Information Act of 2004. 108th Congress (2003–2004) <https://www.congress.gov/bill/108th-congress/house-bill/3872/actions?q=H.R.+3872+%28108%29> accessed 21 July 2022.

[73] Charles R. McManis, 'Database Protection in the Digital Information Age' (n 70) 11. For more on protection of semiconductor chips see Leon Radomsky, 'Sixteen Years after the Passage of the U.S. Semiconductor Chip Protection Act: Is International Protection Working?' (2000) 15 Berkeley Technology Law Journal 1049.

[74] Mark Davison, 'Database Protection: Lessons from Europe, Congress, and WIPO' (2017) 57 Case Western Reserve Law Review 829, 852.

[75] Marshall A. Leaffer, 'Database Protection in the United States is Alive and Well: Comments on Davison' (2007) 2785 Articles by Maurer Faculty 855.

In its report, the U.S. Copyright Office also points out that, in practice, database producers apply a combination of strategies to protect databases against unauthorized use: (1) enhance copyright protection by incorporating creativity into the structure or contents of their databases (thus making the so-called "value-added databases"), (2) rely on the legal instruments offered by contract law (terms and conditions of use, remedies), and (3) employ technological safeguards.[76]

Leaffer elaborates on the legal means available for database protection and stresses that such means encompass causes of action under both federal and state law.

In particular, the Computer Fraud and Abuse Act[77] prohibits access to a protected computer without authorization, or to an extent that exceeds authorized access, imposing civil and criminal liability on the person committing the offence. Leaffer points to *EF Cultural Travel BV v. Explorica, Inc.*[78] as a case demonstrating that the Act has been successful in cases involving databases. According to the facts of the case, Explorica used a specially designed computer program ("scraper") to glean information from EF's website, including travel codes, in order to compete with EF in the field of global tours for high school students. In total, scraper downloaded 60,000 lines of data, which is equivalent to eight telephone directories of information. The court held that "Explorica's wholesale use of EF's travel codes to facilitate gathering EF's prices from its website reeks of use—and, indeed, abuse—of proprietary information that goes beyond any authorized use of EF's website". Not surprisingly, the court decided in favor of the plaintiffs.

Another means of protection under federal law is Section 1201 of the Digital Millennium Copyright Act.[79] Section 1201(a) prohibits circumvention of a technological measure that effectively controls access to a copyright-protected work, which, Leaffer notes, can be useful for protection of electronic databases.

There are also state law remedies that have proven useful in protecting compilations, such as remedies available under contract law, trade secret law, as well as trespass and misappropriation doctrines.

Section 301(a) of the Copyright Act preempts "all legal or equitable rights that are equivalent to any of the exclusive rights within the general scope of copyright as specified by section 106 in works of authorship that are fixed in a tangible medium of expression and come within the subject matter of copyright as specified by sections 102 and 103", therefore "no person is entitled to any such right or equivalent right in any such work under the common law or statutes of any State". One of the main purposes of this provision was to prevent states from giving special protection to works of authorship that Congress has decided should be in the public domain. Nevertheless, case law has shown that these provisions do not affect private contracts, since private contracts create rights and obligations only for the parties to the contracts.

---

[76] U.S. Copyright Office. Report on Legal Protection for Databases, August 1997, 19 <https://www.copyright.gov/reports/db4.pdf> accessed 25 January 2022.

[77] 18 U.S.C. § 1030.

[78] *EF Cultural Travel BV v. Explorica, Inc.*, 274 F.3d 577 (1st Cir. 2001).

[79] 112 Stat. 2860.

Hence, Section 301(a) of the Copyright Act cannot preempt enforcement of such rights.

For instance, in *ProCD v. Zeidenberg*,[80] ProCD, the plaintiff, compiled information from more than 3000 telephone directories into a database software program that it licensed for both personal use and, at a higher price, for commercial use. Matthew Zeidenberg bought a consumer package of the database and formed a corporation to resell the information from the database, at a price lower than ProCD charged its commercial customers. ProCD sued Zeidenberg for breach of the shrinkwrap license conditions. Zeidenberg claimed that the shrinkwrap license was not a valid contract as it merely referenced the license that was inside the package and that Section 301(a) preempted enforcement of ProCD's state law claims. The district court agreed with Zeidenberg holding that the shrinkwrap license was invalid as it did not allow Zeidenberg to review its terms prior to the purchase of the software and that Section 301(a) of the Copyright Act preempts enforcement of shrinkwrap licenses, since they are "within the subject matter of copyright". The Court of Appeals disagreed, noting that the license was valid, as Zeidenberg expressly consented to its terms when running the program for the first time. On the copyright preemption claim, the Court held that rights created by contract are not "equivalent to any of the exclusive rights within the general scope of copyright", since the latter are established by law, restricting the options of persons who are strangers to the author, whereas contracts affect only their parties and do not create exclusive rights. The Court noted that, although Congress possesses power to preempt even the enforcement of contracts about intellectual property, courts usually read preemption clauses to leave private contracts unaffected. Further, the Court concluded that, same as in *Feist*, the database cannot be protected by copyright, but, since a two-party contract is not "equivalent to any of the exclusive rights within the general scope of copyright", shrinkwrap licenses may be enforced.

Trade secret law could grant protection to a database that would not be protected by copyright. For instance, a customer list containing names, addresses, and telephone numbers of customers, in alphabetical order, is not eligible for copyright protection, but can undoubtedly represent a trade secret.

Under the trespass to chattels doctrine, a database, being personal property, can be protected against unauthorized access (interference with the owner's possessory interest) resulting in damage to the owner of the database.

In *eBay v. Bidder's Edge*,[81] Bidder's Edge (BE) was accessing eBay's computer systems with a web crawler copying its auction database. After eBay and BE could not agree on a license agreement and BE ignored eBay's requests to stop connecting with and searching eBay's auction database, eBay filed a claim for injunctive relief on multiple causes of action, including trespass to chattels. Addressing the merits of the trespass claim, the Court noted that trespass to chattels "lies where an intentional interference with the possession of personal property has proximately caused

[80] 86 F.3d 1447.

[81] 100 F. Supp. 2d 1058 (N.D. Cal. 2000).

injury". Referring to the *Thrifty-Tel*[82] case, the Court further observed that the electronic signals sent by BE to retrieve information from eBay's computer system are sufficiently tangible to support a trespass cause of action. Although BE argued that it could not trespass eBay's website because it was publicly accessible, the Court disagreed stating that eBay's servers are private property and eBay does not generally permit the type of automated access made by BE. As to the evidence of injury caused to eBay, the Court considered that if the preliminary injunction relief were denied, it would likely encourage other auction aggregators to crawl the eBay site, potentially to the point of denying effective access to eBay's customers.

BE also appealed based on the copyright preemption theory, however, the Court noted that the right to exclude others from using physical personal property is not equivalent to any rights protected by copyright and therefore constitutes an extra element that makes trespass qualitatively different from a copyright infringement claim. On these grounds, the Court issued a preliminary injunction against BE from using a web crawler or similar device to access eBay's computer systems or networks for the purpose of copying any part of eBay's auction database.

In another case, *Register.com v. Verio*,[83] the Court also upheld the trespass to chattels claim. Verio, a website development company, was accessing Register.com's WHOIS database with search robots and further contacting recent registrants with mail, email, and phone solicitations. The Court considered that Verio's actions resulted in harm (which is a necessary condition for the doctrine to be applied), since if Verio were permitted to continue accessing the database, other Internet service providers would devise similar programs to do the same, and thus the system would be overtaxed and crash.

However, the extension of the trespass to chattels doctrine to the Internet has been highly criticized.[84] Many scholars argue that trespass on the Internet does not cause harm and thus courts have mistakenly applied the trespass to chattels doctrine.[85] According to Burk, it is nearly impossible to recognize trespass to chattels in *Thrifty-Tel*, since the equipment was contacted by electrons, but not touched, damaged, removed, or rendered inoperable.[86] Further, Burk suggests that the property theory of nuisance might be more suitable to address the intrusive activity in

---

[82] *Thrifty-Tel v. Bezenek*, 46 Cal. App. 4th 1559, 1566, 54 Cal. Rptr. 2d 468 (1996). The case concerned unauthorized access by Bezeneks' children to Thrifty-Tel's system and conducting manual random searches for a six-digit authorization code. In this case, the court stated that "the electronic signals generated by the Bezenek boys' activities were sufficiently tangible to support a trespass cause of action".

[83] 356 F.3d 393 (2d Cir. 2004).

[84] In particular, a number of distinguished technology law professors submitted brief amicus curiae, arguing that applying the trespass to chattels doctrine to cyberspace can cause great harm, threatening the foundations of the Internet. See Mark A. Lemley, Brief Amicus Curiae of Technology Law Professors: Ebay v. Bidder's Edge, No. 99-21200 in the U.S. District Court for the Northern District of California (100 F.Supp.2d 1058 (N.D. Cal. 2000)).

[85] See Clifton Merrell, 'Trespass to Chattels in the Age of the Internet' (2002) 80 Washington University Law Review 675.

[86] Dan L. Burk, 'The Trouble with Trespass' (2000) 4 Journal of Small and Emerging Business Law 27.

websites.[87] Not surprisingly, in *Ticketmaster Corp. v. Tickets.com, Inc.*,[88] the Court dismissed the trespass claim disagreeing on the fact that the mere use of a spider to enter a publicly available website to gather information is sufficient to fulfill the harm requirement for trespass to chattels. Moreover, in *Intel Corp. v. Hamidi*,[89] the California Supreme Court disagreed with the court in the *eBay* case that the injury evidence was sufficient for applying the trespass to chattels doctrine. According to the California Supreme Court, the reasoning that BE's conduct, if widely replicated, would likely impair the functioning of eBay's computer systems "would not be a correct statement of California or general American law on this point". By contrast, use of another person's property is actionable only if such use has caused injury.

Lastly, databases can be protected under misappropriation doctrine, although this may not be the first choice of the means of protection for database owners. Leaffer notes that misappropriation doctrine has proven effective "where the material taken by the competitor is time sensitive, the free riding is clear, and injury has occurred".[90] In *Pollster v. Gigmania, Ltd.*,[91] Pollstar was compiling information about upcoming concerts that it allowed to use under a license agreement, whereas Gigmania copied the information onto its website. The court agreed that Gigmania misappropriated the information from Pollstar's database and Pollstar's misappropriation claim was not preempted by copyright law because the information compiled by Pollstar was "hot news".

Therefore, although the U.S. does not have a *sui generis* database right, there are still a number of legal means to provide protection to database owners, which contributes to the U.S. remaining the world leader in the production of databases. As McManis wrote in 2001, there is no domestic policy justification for the U.S. to follow the EU's lead and if the U.S. gave in to the temptation to adopt *sui generis* database protection, it would drive up the prices for databases and the database users would just subsidize a European effort to gain a market share in an industry that the U.S. currently dominates.[92] More than 20 years later, with no *sui generis* database right in the U.S. and its leading position in the database industry,[93] these words appear to have been true.

---

[87] Ibid, 53.

[88] Case No. CV997654HLHVBKX (C.D. Cal. Mar. 7, 2003).

[89] 71 P.3d 296 (Cal. 2003).

[90] Marshall A. Leaffer, 'Database Protection in the United States is Alive and Well: Comments on Davison' (n 75) 858.

[91] 170 F. Supp. 2d 974 (E.D. Cal. 2000).

[92] Charles R. McManis, 'Database Protection in the Digital Information Age' (n 70) 45.

[93] According to the 2022 Gartner Magic Quadrant for Cloud Database Management Systems, a report evaluating the top 20 data and analytics companies in the world, the leaders in the industry are U.S. companies Amazon Web Services, Inc., Microsoft Corporation, Oracle Corporation and Google LLC <https://aws.amazon.com/de/blogs/database/aws-positioned-highest-in-execution-and-furthest-in-vision-in-the-2022-gartner-magic-quadrant-for-cloud-database-management-systems/> accessed 21 February 2023.

2.3 Conclusions

Thus, the *sui generis* regime for protection of databases could not find its way in the U.S., since the opposition to the *sui generis* right has been stronger than in the EU. Given the history of the bills introducing database protection and the opposition from both industry and scholars, it is unlikely that we will see a law on the *sui generis* protection of databases in the U.S. in the near future.

At the same time, it appears that there have been significant prerequisites that have determined the way that the *sui generis* right for database owners would go in the EU and the U.S. In the U.S., even after the *Feist* decision, most databases still met the minimum standard of originality, thus benefiting from copyright protection. Besides, the common law system allows for a number of legal instruments of protection for databases. Although the efficiency of such legal instruments varies, contract law remedies, trade secret law, as well as such common law doctrines as trespass to chattels and misappropriation theory, taken together, form a toolbox for protection for most databases. Whereas in the EU, with the civil law system prevailing, there was a greater need for a statutory right that would be introduced in order to protect unoriginal databases. Besides, harmonization of the different legal regimes of the Member States was one of the main objectives of the novel *sui generis* regime, which, according to the 2018 Evaluation Report, was successfully achieved, as the Database Directive effectively harmonized the national database protection regimes.

Thus, the differing historical, geographic, and legal conditions in the EU and the U.S. have led to different paths in the legal protection of databases. However, it would be overly one-sided to affirm that either of them has been right or wrong, as either approach has its benefits: in the EU, the *sui generis* database right allowed for harmonization of the laws of the Member States and provided legal certainty for database owners, whereas in the U.S., although not enjoying the *sui generis* protection, databases are still protected by other legal instruments, without unnecessary legal restrictions, thus contributing to the growth of the database industry.

Chapter 3
Sui Generis Intellectual Property Protection for Designs

Design is a part of visual communication, which has always played an important role in the society. For instance, when the UK textile industry was thriving, it was the designs applied to fabrics that were perceived to be of particular value.[1] As Hudson notes, in the past century the public has become even more conscious of design and appearance in all manner of things in everyday life, from kitchenware to automobiles.[2] Design gives a product an aesthetic aspect and is thus an important element in the product's value. The legal protection of designs encourages creativity and assists the establishment of industries, and is therefore in the interest of all countries.[3]

Historically, designs have been protected by copyright, a specific design regime, or a cumulation of both. Moreover, design rights are considered a "prime example" of a *sui generis* right with "a tumultuous legislative history since its inception in the eighteenth century".[4]

In the United Kingdom, the first statute to explicitly provide protection for designs was the Calico Printers' Act of 1787, which was further repealed by the Ornamental Designs Act of 1842.[5] At the same time, the criticism of the Victorian British patent system as being overly complex and costly yielded the introduction of the

[1] Alexander Carter-Silk and Michelle Lewiston, 'The Development of Design Law - Past and Future: From History to Policy' [2012] 15 The Intellectual Property Office <https://assets.publishing.service.gov.uk/government/uploads/system/uploads/attachment_data/file/310380/ipresearch-designlaw-201207.pdf> accessed 30 November 2021.

[2] Thomas B. Hudson, 'A Brief History of the Development of Design Patent Protection in the United States' (1948) 30 Journal of the Patent Office Society 380.

[3] WIPO and BIRPI. Model Law for Developing Countries on Industrial Designs <https://www.wipo.int/edocs/pubdocs/en/wipo_pub_808.pdf> accessed 19 August 2022.

[4] Uma Suthersanen, 'Function, Art and Fashion: Do We Need the EU Design Law?' 88/2011 Queen Mary School of Law Legal Studies Research Paper <https://papers.ssrn.com/sol3/papers.cfm?abstract_id=1945142> accessed 2 November 2021.

[5] Alexander Carter-Silk and Michelle Lewiston, 'The Development of Design Law - Past and Future: From History to Policy' [2012] 15 The Intellectual Property

I. Kazeeva, *Sui Generis Intellectual Property Protection*, Perspectives in Law, Business and Innovation, https://doi.org/10.1007/978-981-99-8897-6_3

Utility Designs Act of 1843.[6] The Ornamental Designs Act protected the ornamental designs, and the Utility Designs Act protected the designs for the shape or configuration of useful articles of manufacture, thus introducing a distinction between ornamental and non-ornamental designs. Both regimes were administered by the Designs Registry, part of the Board of Trade, that later fell under the jurisdiction of the Patent Office.[7]

Describing the history of the British design and copyright laws, Bently divides it into three periods. The first is the period of quiet coexistence (1787–1911) when design laws sat alongside copyright regimes. The second period is that of demarcation (1912–1968) during which attempts were made to ensure that material eligible for protection under registered design regime was excluded from copyright protection. The current period of cumulation (1968-present) is being characterized by partial overlap and systemic coordination between the two legal regimes.[8]

In France, some of the first design laws were the Letters Patent (*lettres patentes*) of 1737 and the King's Council decision of 1744 granting protection for creations of the silk industries of Lyon. The Copyright Act of 1902 established the theory of the unity of art (*unité de l'art*) meaning that all kinds of work, pure art as well as applied art, could benefit from the protection afforded by copyright. France became the only country whose legislation enabled total cumulation, i.e., assimilation of the protection requirements of one law with that of the other, granting double protection to one single industrial creation: that of copyright and of specific law on industrial designs and models. Although, the recent case law tends to be turning away from absolute cumulation towards one that is partial, or reasoned.[9]

In the United States, the design patent regime was introduced in the 1842 Act that granted the design patent rightholders the exclusive right to make, use, and sell their novel designs for a term of seven years. The 1842 Act reflected the main concern pursued by the Congress, particularly to grant the American manufacturers the same intellectual property rights as enjoyed by their competitors under the British law. Initially, the protectable subject matter under copyright and design patent law did not overlap, but further development of copyright law created a potential for conflict, which resulted in the requirement to elect between design patent and copyright law

Office <https://assets.publishing.service.gov.uk/government/uploads/system/uploads/attachment_data/file/310380/ipresearch-designlaw-201207.pdf> accessed 30 November 2021.

[6] See Mark D. Janis, 'Second Tier Patent Protection' (1999) 40 Harvard International Law Journal 151, 156; Uma Suthersanen, 'Utility models: Do they really serve national innovation strategies?' 274/2018 Queen Mary School of Law Legal Studies Research Paper <https://papers.ssrn.com/sol3/papers.cfm?abstract_id=3139963> accessed 4 November 2021.

[7] The National Archives. Intellectual property: registered designs 1839–1991 <https://www.nationalarchives.gov.uk/help-with-your-research/research-guides/registered-designs-1839-1991/> accessed 29 November 2021.

[8] Lionel Bently, 'The Design/Copyright Conflict in the United Kingdom: a History' in Estelle Derclaye (ed), *The Copyright/Design Interface: Past, Present and Future* (Cambridge University Press 2018) 171.

[9] Anne-Emmanuelle Kahn, 'The Copyright/Design Interface in France' in Estelle Derclaye (ed), *The Copyright/Design Interface: Past, Present and Future* (Cambridge University Press 2018) 7.

protection in the early twentieth century. However, over time, the U.S. design patent law has demarcated from copyright, thus both types of legal protection can be applied for the same design.[10]

At the international level, the first treaties establishing the system for registration of industrial designs (the Hague System) were made in the first part of the twentieth century, namely the 1925 Hague Agreement and the 1934 London Act,[11] further replaced by the 1960 Hague Agreement and 1999 Geneva Act, forming the backbone of the WIPO's Hague System.[12]

Under the Paris Convention for the Protection of Industrial Property, industrial designs fall within the scope of industrial property (Article 1(2)). Furthermore, it requires that industrial designs be protected in all the countries of the Union (Article 5*quinquies*).

Under the TRIPS Agreement, its members should provide for the protection of independently created industrial designs that are new or original (Article 25(1)). With regard to textile designs, members shall be free to meet this obligation through industrial design law or through copyright law (Article 25(2)).

Efforts at creating a *sui generis* right for design protection at international level were started by the Association Litteraire et Artistique Internationale in 1956, when it was decided that the issue should be studied by international organizations.[13] In the 1960s, the International Association for the Protection of Intellectual Property made a number of observations in its Resolution "International protection of works of applied art, designs and models" with respect to revising the Hague agreement. At the congresses in the 1980s, the AIPPI confirmed the definition of the object of protection of a design, resolving that a model of which the characteristics are dictated solely by its function (technical needs) should not be suitable for design protection. Finally, at the Seoul congress in 2012, the AIPPI studied the interplay between design and copyright protection for industrial products advocating for cumulative protection between copyright and design rights, except for the cases when the shape or appearance of the product is dictated exclusively by functional considerations.[14]

In 1970, the United International Bureaux for the Protection of Intellectual Property (BIRPI) and WIPO, gradually replacing BIRPI since April 1970, drew up

---

[10] Jason J. Du Mont and Mark D. Janis, 'US Design Patent Law: a Historical Look at the Design Patent/Copyright Interface' in Estelle Derclaye (ed), *The Copyright/Design Interface: Past, Present and Future* (Cambridge University Press 2018) 341.

[11] WIPO. Hague Agreement Concerning the International Registration of Industrial Designs. Historical archives <https://www.wipo.int/treaties/en/registration/hague/index.html#accordion__collapse__02_a> accessed 18 August 2022.

[12] WIPO. Hague System Legal Texts <https://www.wipo.int/hague/en/legal_texts/> accessed 20 August 2022.

[13] Estelle Derclaye, 'A Model Copyright/Design Interface: Not an Impossible and Undesirable Task?' in Estelle Derclaye (ed), *The Copyright/Design Interface: Past, Present and Future* (Cambridge University Press 2018) 421.

[14] AIPPI. Study Guidelines 2016 – Study Question (Designs) Requirements for protection of designs <http://www.aippi.ch/wp-content/uploads/2018/01/AIPPI-Milan-Designs-Guidelines-FINAL-1.pdf> accessed 18 August 2022.

a Model Law for Developing Countries on Industrial Designs,[15] mentioning that protection of industrial designs is of special importance for developing countries, since these countries are extremely rich in traditional art and folklore. The Model Law defines industrial design as "any composition of lines or colors or any three-dimensional form, whether or not associated with lines or colors, … provided that such composition or form gives a special appearance to a product of industry or handicraft and can serve as a pattern for a product of industry or handicraft" (Section 2). In order to qualify for protection, an industrial design must be new (Section 3).

However, since the obligations imposed by international treaties are very general and flexible and the Model Law is optional, each jurisdiction decides on its own whether designs should be provided with a special form of intellectual property legal protection.

3.1 Legal Protection of Designs in the EU

The importance of legal protection of designs was realized early by the EU. Only two years after the Treaty of Rome, in 1959, the six original Member States, namely, Belgium, France, Germany, Italy, Luxembourg, and the Netherlands, set up three working parties on patents, trademarks, and designs. In its report delivered in 1962, the working group on designs emphasized the immense difficulty in adopting uniform design rules at the Community level due to substantial differences in the national legal regimes of the Member States, particularly in the definition of design, criteria and term of protection, and the overlap between design and other intellectual property rights.[16]

In the 1980s, a number of ECJ cases have further demonstrated the need for harmonization of designs laws. In *Keurkoop v Nancy Kean Gifts*,[17] Nancy Kean Gifts registered a design of a ladies' handbag with the Benelux Design Office, whereas Keurkoop B. V. was selling a similar design in the Netherlands, imported from Germany. The ECJ held that "the proprietor of a right to a design acquired under the legislation of a Member State may prevent the importation of products from another Member State which are identical in appearance to the design which has been filed, provided that the products in question have not been put into circulation in the other Member States by, or with the consent of, the proprietor of a right". The ECJ referred to *Keurkoop v. Nancy Kean Gifts* in two further cases, *Consorzio*

[15] WIPO and BIRPI. Model Law for Developing Countries on Industrial Designs <https://www.wipo.int/publications/en/details.jsp?id=3173&plang=EN> accessed 19 August 2022.

[16] Legal review on industrial design protection in Europe. Under the contract with the Directorate General Internal Market, Industry, Entrepreneurship and SMEs (MARKT2014/083/D). Final Report—15 April 2016 <https://op.europa.eu/en/publication-detail/-/publication/43fd4a5c-6c26-4639-ac9a-281ab57687de> accessed 11 September 2022.

[17] Case C-144/81 *Keurkoop BV v Nancy Kean Gifts BV* [1982] ECR 02853.

Italiano and Maxicar v. Renault[18] and *Volvo v. Erik Veng*,[19] reiterating that national design rights could, in certain circumstances, segment the internal market. Thus, as David Stone notes, it was obvious that without harmonization of national design laws, the internal market would remain open to segmentation.[20]

By the 1990s, design laws harmonization was obviously behind as compared to the progress made in harmonizing patent and trademark laws. In 1991, the Commission issued the Green Paper on the legal protection of industrial design,[21] where it pointed out that different intellectual property laws act as barriers to the free circulation of goods, and the single Community market will become a reality for European design industries only if the territorial effect and limitations of the national intellectual property laws are replaced by Community-wide legislation. Community-wide protection, the Green Paper concluded, needs to be introduced by way of a Regulation, should be based on registration and last five years, renewable to a maximum of 25 years. One of the main conclusions of the Green Paper is the condition of protection of a design, being that the design is distinct from designs known to the circles specialized in the sector concerned operating in the Community and by the overall impression that it creates in the eyes of the public. The proprietor of the Community Design, according to the Green Paper, should have the exclusive right to prevent any third party not having his consent from making, offering, putting on the market, or using a product to which the same design or a substantially similar design is applied.

Following the publication of the Green Paper, the Commission held consultations with the design industry, and, in 1993, the Commission adopted a Proposal for a European Parliament and Council Regulation on the Community Design[22] and a Proposal for a European Parliament and Council Directive on the legal protection of designs.[23]

The Directive on the legal protection of designs[24] (Design Directive) was finally adopted on 13 October 1998. One of its main objectives was harmonizing national design laws of the Member States in order to ensure the smooth functioning of the internal market (Recital 3). However, procedural provisions concerning registration, renewal, and invalidation of design rights, as well as provisions on sanctions, remedies, and enforcement should, according to the Directive, be left to national law

[18] Case C-53/87 *Consorzio italiano della componentistica di ricambio per autoveicoli and Maxicar v Régie nationale des usines Renault* [1988] ECR 06039.

[19] Case C-238/87 *AB Volvo v Erik Veng (UK) Ltd* [1988] ECR 06211.

[20] David Stone, 'European Union Design Law: A Practitioners' Guide' (Oxford University Press 2016).

[21] Commission of the European Communities. Green Paper on the legal protection of industrial design. Working document of the services of the Commission. III/F/5131/91-EN, June 1991.

[22] Proposal for a European Parliament and Council Regulation on the Community Design. COM/93/342FINAL—COD 463.

[23] Proposal for a European Parliament and Council Directive on the legal protection of designs 1993/0464/COD.

[24] Directive 98/71/EC of the European Parliament and of the Council of 13 October 1998 on the legal protection of designs [1998] OJ L 289/28.

(Recitals 5 and 6). Excluded from the application of the Directive are also unregistered design rights, trade marks or other distinctive signs, patents and utility models, typefaces, civil liability or unfair competition (Article 16). Thus, the Design Directive only aims to harmonize substantive registered design law, in particular protectable subject matter, conditions of protection, scope of protection, validity.

The provisions of the Design Directive apply to design rights registered in the Member States, including those registered under the Benelux system, and those registered under the WIPO's Hague System having effect in a Member State, as well as applications for the respective design rights (Article 2).

The Design Directive requires Member States to protect a design by registration to the extent that it is new and has individual character (Article 3). The novelty criterion is fulfilled if no identical design has been made available to the public before the date of filing of the application for registration (Article 4). Individual character means that the overall impression a design produces on the informed user differs from the overall impression produced on such a user by any design which has been made available to the public before the date of filing of the application for registration (Article 5). The rightholder has an exclusive right to use the protected design and to prevent any third party not having his consent from using it, meaning, in particular making, offering, putting on the market, importing, exporting a product in which the design is incorporated or to which it is applied (Article 12). The term of protection shall be five years, renewable by periods of five years each, up to a total term of 25 years (Article 10).

After a number of revisions since the 1993 Proposal, the Regulation on Community designs[25] (Design Regulation) was adopted in 2001. One year later, two other regulations were issued: the Implementing Regulation,[26] covering the procedure on registration, administration, invalidation of Community designs, and the Fees Regulation,[27] setting forth the fees charged for the services related to Community designs.

The main purpose of the Design Regulation was to provide a Community-wide design right that would facilitate the free flow of goods within the internal market. Harmonization of design law with the Design Directive alone would just align the common denominators and would have retained the territorial nature of design rights, leading to segmentation of internal market. Therefore, a new European design legal instrument had to be introduced.[28]

The Design Regulation creates two EU-wide *sui generis* design rights: (1) the unregistered Community design right (UCD), an anti-copying right with term of protection of three years from the date the design was first made available to the

[25] Council Regulation (EC) No 6/2002 of 12 December 2001 on Community designs [2001] OJ 3/1.

[26] Commission Regulation (EC) 2245/2002 of 21 October 2002 implementing Council Regulation (EC) 6/2002 on Community designs [2002] OJ L341/28.

[27] Commission Regulation (EC) 2246/2002 of 16 December 2002 on the fees payable to the Office for Harmonization in the Internal Market (Trade Marks and Designs) in respect of the registration of Community designs [2002] OJ L341/54.

[28] Legal review on industrial design protection in Europe (n 16) 25.

public, and (b) the registered Community design right (RCD), an exclusive right to use a design and to prevent any third party not having a rightholder's consent from using it, with the term of protection of five years (renewable up to 25 years) (Articles 1, 11, 12, and 19). Same as under the Design Directive, in order to be protected by Community design, a design should be new and have individual character (Article 4). The novelty criterion is satisfied if no identical design has been made available to the public: in case of UCD, before the date on which the design has first been made available to the public, and, in case of RCD, before the date of filing of the application for registration of the design (Article 5).

Both the Design Directive and Design Regulation provide for the same definition of "design", meaning the appearance of the whole or a part of a product resulting from the features of, in particular the lines, contours, colors, shape, texture, and/or materials of the product itself and/or its ornamentation (Articles 1 and 3, respectively). The term "product" is defined meaning any industrial or handicraft item, including, *inter alia*, parts intended to be assembled into a complex product, packaging, get-up, graphic symbols, and typographic typefaces, but excluding computer programs. Suthersanen suggests that "get-up" will presumably extend to restaurant and window interiors and displays, and one can even stretch the concept of product design to environmental design and landscape design, including props and costumes used for a film set.[29]

Both legal instruments also exclude from protection designs that are dictated solely by their technical function (Articles 7 and 8, respectively) and provide for common limitations of the design rights, particularly for private use, experimental purposes, teaching, etc. (Articles 13 and 20).

Both the Design Directive and Design Regulation stress that, in the absence of complete harmonization of copyright law, it is important to ensure cumulation of registered design protection law and copyright law (principle of cumulation), thus a design protected by a design right registered in a Member State should also be eligible for protection under the law of copyright of that state (Article 17 of the Design Directive, Article 96 of the Design Regulation). According to Stone, the intention appears to have been to ensure that Member States do not limit copyright law where design protection is available.[30] However, in case *Cofemel - Sociedade de Vestuário, SA v G-Star Raw CV*,[31] the ECJ drew the line between design and copyright protection. The Court noted that protection of designs, on the one hand, and copyright protection, on the other hand, pursue different objectives and are subject to distinct rules. The purpose of design protection is to protect subject matter which, while being new and distinctive, is functional and liable to be mass-produced. Design protection is applicable for a limited time, ensuring a return on the investment necessary for the creation and production of that subject matter without excessively restricting competition. At the same time, copyright protection is reserved to subject matter that merits being classified as works (any original subject matter constituting

[29] Uma Suthersanen, 'Function, Art and Fashion: Do We Need the EU Design Law?' (n 4).

[30] David Stone, 'European Union Design Law: A Practitioners' Guide' (n 20) 81.

[31] Case C-683/17 *Cofemel - Sociedade de Vestuário, SA v G-Star Raw CV* [2019] Court Reports—general.

the expression of its author's own intellectual creation) and is therefore granted for a significantly longer period of time. Thus, concurrent protection by both design and copyright laws can be envisaged only in certain situations, so as not to undermine the respective objectives and effectiveness of either form of protection.

According to the EUIPO Statistics for Community Designs, the number of applications for RCD has been growing from 23,196 in 2013 to 32,666 in 2021 and the number of RCDs received has been growing each year during this period from 86,850 in 2013 to 101,173 in 2021 (as one filed RCD application can have multiple designs).[32] As noted in the Evaluation of EU Legislation on Design Protection published by the European Commission in 2020,[33] "the steady increase in the number of design applications filed with the EUIPO proves both the success of the Community design system and the rising importance companies give to protecting their designs".

Thus, the *sui generis* design rights have been widely used in the EU serving the needs of multiple design industries. However, many scholars cast doubt on the effectiveness of the regime and question whether the *sui generis* regime has solved the dilemma of design legal protection.

Suthersanen observes that, although the EU *sui generis* design regime was to be a new and contrasting approach to the legal protection of designs, "where designs would be protected as both industrial property (registration) or as copyright (unregistered rights)", with cumulative protection by national copyright law, this approach has shown some fundamental flaws. In particular, she writes, scholars and practitioners remain skeptical over the real use of the UCD. Fashion and consumer goods industries argued for a copyright or unfair competition protection, particularly taking into account the cyclical nature of products and consumer taste. However, the short-lived products industries were offered an anti-copying right with an extremely restrictive scope of protection. Also, since "subject matter defies strict definitional parameters", it is difficult to draw the line between various forms of protection, especially where design incorporates both artistic and functional features. Suthersanen concludes that "the current paradox of a complicated, art/function-led multi-tiered protection system does lead one naturally to question the very rationale of *sui generis* design law". One of the suggestions that she makes is using the misappropriation laws in order to protect designs.[34]

Philipps expresses a similar view noting that "a quick survey of design law reveals the degree of chaos to which this topic has sunk": designs may be protected by almost all kinds of intellectual property legal instruments, including *sui generis* rights, may be registered and unregistered, with international treaties providing little guidance on their legal protection. And even if protection is granted, its real value is seriously

[32] EUIPO Statistics for Community Designs. 2003-01 to 2022-07 Evolution <https://euipo.europa.eu/tunnel-web/secure/webdav/guest/document_library/contentPdfs/about_euipo/the_office/statistics-of-community-designs_en.pdf> accessed 1 September 2022.

[33] European Commission. Evaluation of EU legislation on design protection <https://ec.europa.eu/docsroom/documents/43705> accessed 16 September 2022.

[34] Uma Suthersanen, 'Function, Art and Fashion: Do We Need the EU Design Law?' (n 4).

doubted, since, with both registered and unregistered design rights, the scope of protection is so narrow that a competitor can make minor changes and sell a similar product without fear of legal action.[35]

However, the EU *sui generis* design regime still provides an outstanding approach to design legal protection and has also helped achieve an important goal that the EU legislators were facing, particularly harmonization of the national design laws and facilitating the free circulation of goods that is essential for the internal market. As noted by Derclaye, the EU design law is the most harmonized regional design regime in the world, which is an amazing achievement of the EU legislators given that some EU countries historically paid a lot of attention to intellectual property protection of designs (France, Italy) and some EU countries had no design laws at all (Greece).[36]

The 2020 Evaluation of EU Legislation on Design Protection stressed that the main goals of the *sui generis* design rights in the EU were to promote "a single market and an undistorted competition regime for products embodying designs". The conducted studies have shown that the introduced *sui generis* regime has been broadly successful in reaching these goals. According to the evaluation, the *sui generis* rights provide "access to simple and affordable design protection by making it significantly easier and less costly to obtain a registered design right that is valid across the whole EU". The evaluation concludes that "it is likely that without EU legislation on design protection, big differences between national laws would have remained, with the result that the internal market for goods embodying designs would remain fragmented and distorted". At the same time, the evaluation also reported a number of weak points of the design regime, namely only partial harmonization of the provisions on component parts used for repair of complex products and unclear interaction with copyright law, in particular the principle of cumulation,—an issue that was also broadly discussed by the scholars, as noted above.

However, despite the flaws indicated both by scholars and in the evaluation, the EU *sui generis* design regime remains an outstanding example of harmonization of national design laws, providing legal certainty to designers of multiple industries in the EU. Such example of legal certainty that could be provided to designers, along with the high numbers of applications for RCDs and granted RCDs, make the supporters of a *sui generis* design protection in the U.S. view the EU *sui generis* designs rights as a model that the U.S. should follow.[37]

[35] Jeremy Phillips, 'Editorial:The great design conundrum' (2011) 6(8) Journal of Intellectual Property Law & Practice 507.

[36] Estelle Derclaye, 'A Model Copyright/Design Interface: Not an Impossible and Undesirable Task?' in Estelle Derclaye (ed), *The Copyright/Design Interface: Past, Present and Future* (Cambridge University Press 2018) 421, 425–426.

[37] See, e.g., Tiffany Mahmood, 'Design Law in the United States as Compared to the European Community Design System: What Do We Need to Fix?' (2015) 24 Fordham Intellectual Property, Media and Entertainment Law Journal 555.

3.2 Legal Protection of Designs in the U.S.

In the U.S., designs can generally be protected by copyright, design patent, and trademark law.

Under copyright law, design of a useful article can be protected as a pictorial, graphic, and sculptural work, "only if, and only to the extent that, such design incorporates pictorial, graphic, or sculptural features that can be identified separately from, and are capable of existing independently of, the utilitarian aspects of the article". "Pictorial, graphic, and sculptural works" include two-dimensional and three-dimensional works of fine, graphic, and applied art, photographs, prints and art reproductions, maps, globes, charts, diagrams, models, and technical drawings, including architectural plans. Whereas a "useful article" is an article having an intrinsic utilitarian function that is not merely to portray the appearance of the article or to convey information.[38]

Design of a useful article came under protection of copyright law since the 1976 Copyright Act,[39] repealing the Copyright Act of 1909.[40] The major case affecting the provisions on designs was *Mazer v. Stein*,[41] where the Court held that the statuettes used as bases for electric lamps, although being eligible for design patent protection, were also copyrightable. The Court drew the line between patent and copyright protection by saying that "unlike a patent, a copyright gives no exclusive right to the art disclosed; protection is given only to the expression of the idea – not the idea itself". The Court concluded that the intended use or use in industry of an article eligible for copyright does not bar or invalidate its registration, and the subsequent registration of copyright for a work of art comprising an element in a manufactured article is not a misuse of copyright.

Designs, and particularly clothing designs, were further granted copyright protection after the *Star Athletica, LLC v. Varsity Brands, Inc.*[42] case. Deciding on the copyrightability of the designs of cheerleading uniforms consisting of various lines, chevrons, and colorful shapes, the Court held that copyright law only protects creative elements that are separable from a useful article, thus creating the so-called "separability" test. In *Kieselstein-Cord v. Accessories by Pearl, Inc.*,[43] the belt buckles, although being useful articles, were found copyrightable, since primary ornamental aspects of the Vaquero and Winchester buckles, created by a designer inspired by the Spanish architecture and the antique rifle, respectively, were conceptually separable from their subsidiary utilitarian function.

---

38 17 U.S.C. § 101.

39 90 Stat. 2541.

40 35 Stat. 1075.

41 347 U.S. 201 (1954).

42 580 U.S. ___ (2017).

43 632 F.2d 989 (1980).

The protection available under the U.S. patent law comes in the form of design patents.[44] Design patents were introduced in 1842, several decades after France and the UK had enacted their design laws. According to the report submitted to the 27th Congress by the Commissioner of Patents Ellsworth in 1841, people visiting the Patent Office learned with astonishment that no protection was available for new and original designs of articles of manufacture, as designs could be freely copied. The 1842 Act provided patent protection for any new and original design for an article of manufacture, printing of fabrics, busts, statutes, etc.[45]

As to the question why legal protection for designs was granted under the patent laws instead of copyright laws, Hudson names two main reasons. First, the subject matter of protection, being manufactured articles of commerce, were logically more closely related to patents rather than to the copyright field. Second, the suggestion for the law came from the Commissioner of Patents.[46]

Design patent may be granted to the inventor of any new, original, and ornamental design for an article of manufacture.[47] General provisions on patents for inventions also apply to design patents.[48] Thus, a design, in order to gain protection, should be non-obvious to a person having ordinary skill in the art.[49] Patents for designs shall be granted for the term of fifteen years from the date of grant.[50]

In *Gorham Company v. White*,[51] the Supreme Court emphasized that "it is the appearance itself … that constitutes mainly, if not entirely, the contribution to the public which the law deems worthy of recompense", thus drawing a clear line between design patents and utility patents. Regarding the identity test of a design used to determine infringement, the Court concluded that it is the sameness of effect of an article of manufacture upon the eye of an ordinary observer rather than the eye of an expert, so that if the "resemblance is such as to deceive such an observer, inducing him to purchase one supposing it to be the other, the first one patented is infringed by the other". The design patent infringement test also applies to design patent anticipation,[52] because "that which infringes, if later, would anticipate, if earlier".[53] The "ornamental" requirement of the design patent was commented upon in *Seiko Epson Corporation v. Nu-Kote International, Inc.*,[54] where the court explained it as

---

[44] Regan E. Keebaugh, 'Intellectual Property and the Protection of Industrial Design: Are Sui Generis Protection Measures the Answer to Vocal Opponents and a Reluctant Congress?' (2005) 13 Journal of Intellectual Property Law 255, 260.

[45] Thomas B. Hudson, 'A Brief History of the Development of Design Patent Protection in the United States' (n 2).

[46] Ibid 382–383.

[47] 35 U.S.C. § 171(a).

[48] 35 U.S. Code § 171(b).

[49] 35 U.S. Code § 103.

[50] 35 U.S. Code § 173.

[51] 81 U.S. (14 Wall.) 511 (1872).

[52] *Door-Master Corporation v. Yorktowne, Inc.*, 256 F.3d 1308, 1312–13 (Fed. Cir. 2001).

[53] *Peters v. Active Manufacturing Co.*, 129 U.S. 530, 9 S. Ct. 389 (1889).

[54] 190 F.3d 1360, 1368 (Fed. Cir. 1999).

meaning "that the design must not be governed solely by function, i.e., that this is not the only possible form of the article that could perform its function". The court also noted that the design need not be aesthetically pleasing.

The legal protection of trademark and trade dress serves the purpose of preventing consumer deception and unfair competition. Section 43(a) of the Lanham Act[55] has been widely applied for the protection of product designs. The U.S. courts have universally applied the requirement for distinctiveness of a trade dress, in order for it to be protected under Section 43(a), since without distinctiveness the trade dress would not cause confusion as to the origin of the goods. Distinctiveness can be achieved in two ways: (1) if a trade dress is inherently distinctive, meaning its intrinsic nature serves to identify a particular source, or (2) if it has developed secondary meaning. In *Two Pesos, Inc. v. Taco Cabana, Inc.*,[56] the Supreme Court confirmed that the trade dress of Taco Cabana restaurants, created with the festive eating atmosphere having interior dining and patio areas decorated with artifacts, bright colors, and murals, was inherently distinctive and thus protectable under Section 43(a) without showing that such trade dress has acquired a secondary meaning, "since such trade dress itself is capable of identifying products or services as coming from a specific source". In a different case, *Wal-Mart Stores, Inc. v. Samara Brothers, Inc.*,[57] the Supreme Court distinguished product packaging from product design and held that a product design is distinctive, and therefore protectable, only upon proof of secondary meaning. Notably, the Court also remarked that availability of other legal protections, particularly design patent and copyright, greatly reduces any harm to the producer that might ensue from the Court's conclusion that a product design cannot be protected under Section 43(a) without proof of secondary meaning.

With no *sui generis* regime available for designs, design patent is being considered the closest intellectual property protection regime in the U.S. to the Community designs in the EU, as well as "probably the strongest form of protection against knock-offs".[58] At the same time, some scholars believe that, with the evolvement of copyright and trademark laws, the goals of the design patent system can be more appropriately achieved with copyright and trademark protection, and thus design patents should be eliminated.[59] However, design patents are widely used in practice, and companies continue to significantly rely on design patents. This has been demonstrated in the patent lawsuits between Apple Inc. and Samsung Electronics Co., where Apple initially chose to rely on a small number of design patents (out of

[55] 15 U.S. Code § 1125.

[56] 505 U.S. 763 (1992).

[57] 529 U.S. 205, 120 S. Ct. 1339 (2000).

[58] Tiffany Mahmood, 'Design Law in the United States as Compared to the European Community Design System: What Do We Need to Fix?' (2015) 24 Fordham Intellectual Property, Media and Entertainment Law Journal 555.

[59] Daniel H. Brean, 'Enough is Enough: Time to Eliminate Design Patents and Rely on More Appropriate Copyright and Trademark Protection for Product Designs' (2008) 16 Texas Intellectual Property Law Journal 325.

more than 1,300 patents in mobile electronics technology of its patent portfolio) that covered "simple but elegant design of the iPhone form".[60]

Statistically, the number of applications and grants of design patents has been steadily growing over the years, amounting to 29,059, 39,097 and 47,838 applications for design patents in 2010, 2015 and 2020, and 22,799, 25,986 and 34,877 grants, respectively.[61] Comparing to the number of registered designs in the EU, these numbers still remain insignificant. According to the EUIPO Statistics for Community Designs, the total number of designs received from 2013 to 2022 amounts to 893,863.[62] Whereas the total number of granted design patents in the U.S. for the period from 2011 to 2020 amounts to 276,329. Thus, the number of registered designs in the EU equals to three times the amount of design patents granted in the U.S. over a mostly overlapping 10-year period. Therefore, a statement made more than thirty years ago that "the great bulk of industrial design is simply not protectable by design patents"[63] still appears to be true.

In general, the U.S. system for the protection of designs remains very fragmented. Although such fragmented character allows for flexibility, it is often acknowledged that there is no federal statute suited to the needs of designers and design owners.[64] Indeed, the slow process of acquiring a design patent at the USPTO is incompatible with the short lifecycles of designs. Proof of secondary meaning as a requirement for trademark protection makes this form of legal protection available only for well-known brands and designs. As to copyright law, the useful article doctrine creates uncertainty for designers as to whether their design will be granted protection or not.

For these reasons, many scholars and practitioners believe that designs are still not adequately protected with the available instruments of intellectual property law and that the U.S. needs a *sui generis* system similar to the one introduced in the EU.[65]

However, the only field where the efforts of the supporters of a *sui generis* regime for designs have been successful so far is the vessel hull design.[66] The trigger for

---

[60] Wael Zohn, 'Examining the Role of Patent Quality in Large-Scale "Patent War" Litigation. A Historical Comparison and Proposal for a Restorative U.S. Patent System' (Nomos Verlagsgesellschaft mbH 2018) <https://www.jstor.org/stable/j.ctv941rps.9> accessed 9 September 2022.

[61] USPTO. Patent Technology Monitoring Team (PTMT). U.S. Patent Statistics Chart Calendar Years 1963–2020 <https://www.uspto.gov/web/offices/ac/ido/oeip/taf/us_stat.htm> accessed 1 September 2022.

[62] EUIPO Statistics for Community Designs. 2003–01 to 2022–07 Evolution <https://euipo.europa.eu/tunnel-web/secure/webdav/guest/document_library/contentPdfs/about_euipo/the_office/statistics-of-community-designs_en.pdf> accessed 1 September 2022.

[63] See Industrial Innovation and Technology Act: Hearings on S. 791 Before the Subcommittee on Patents, Copyrights and Trademarks of the Senate Comm. on the Judiciary, 100th Cong., 1st Sess. 8–9 (1987) (statement of Hon. Giles S. Rich).

[64] Ibid.

[65] See, e.g., Tiffany Mahmood, 'Design Law in the United States as Compared to the European Community Design System: What Do We Need to Fix?' (2015) 24 Fordham Intellectual Property, Media and Entertainment Law Journal 555.

[66] Regan E. Keebaugh, 'Intellectual Property and the Protection of Industrial Design: Are Sui Generis Protection Measures the Answer to Vocal Opponents and a Reluctant Congress?' (n 44).

vessel hull design protection was the case *Bonito Boats Inc. v. Thunder Craft Boats Inc.*[67] heard before the U.S. Supreme Court. Bonito Boats Inc. sued Thunder Craft Boats Inc. for using direct molding process to duplicate the fiberglass hull in violation of a Florida statute enacted several years after Bonito had created this hull design for a recreational boat. The Florida Circuit Court found that the statute conflicted with federal patent law, which was affirmed by the upper courts, including the U.S. Supreme Court. The decision created a lobbying backlash from the recreational boat manufacturing industry, which resulted in introducing the *sui generis* protection for boat hull designs.[68]

The Vessel Hull Design Protection Act (VHDPA) was based on the general design bill that had been considered by Congress several times without enactment.[69] The VHDPA was enacted as Chapter 13 to Title 17 of the U.S. Code as part of the Digital Millennium Copyright Act of 1998.[70] However, as noted in the 2003 Report prepared by the U.S. Copyright Office and the USPTO, these provisions do not provide copyright protection, but rather establish a *sui generis* protection for original designs of vessel hulls.[71] The VHDPA provides for a ten-year term of protection of original designs of vessel hulls which make a vessel attractive or distinctive in appearance to the purchasing or using public. Owners of protected designs are granted exclusive rights to make, have made, import, sell, or distribute for sale or for use in trade any useful article embodying protected designs. Application for design registration should be made within two years after the date on which the design is first made public.[72] For the purposes of the VHDPA, "vessel" is a craft designed to navigate on water, but does not include any such craft that exceeds 200 feet in length, and a "hull" is the frame or body of a vessel, including the deck, exclusive of masts, sails, yards, and rigging (Section 1201). A vessel hull design shall not be subject to protection if (1) it is not original, (2) staple or commonplace, (3) dictated solely by a utilitarian function of the article that embodies it, or (4) embodied in a useful article that was made public by the designer or owner more than one year before the date of application for registration (Section 1202).

According to Fryer, the VHDPA does not provide copyright protection, but rather a *sui generis* form of protection for both the ornamental appearance and utilitarian

[67] 489 U.S. 141 (1989).

[68] Bradley J. Olson, 'The Vessel Hull Design Protection Act of 1998: is it still afloat?' (2006) 1(11) Journal of Intellectual Property Law & Practice.

[69] William T. Fryer III, 'Vessel Hull Design Protection Act. Introductory Report and Legislative History Resources' (1998) Fryer Institute on Intellectual Property Law < https://www.fryer.com/vhdparp.htm > accessed 4 September 2022.

[70] 112 Stat. 2860.

[71] U.S. Copyright Office and USPTO. The Vessel Hull Design Protection Act: Overview and Analysis (2003) <https://www.copyright.gov/reports/vhdpa-report.pdf> accessed 22 December 2022.

[72] Summary: H.R.2696 — 105th Congress (1997–1998) <https://www.congress.gov/bill/105th-congress/house-bill/2696> accessed 3 September 2022.

function of a vessel hull.[73] Thus, with one registration under the VHDPA, the boat manufacturer can achieve such a level of protection for his design as could be achieved only through a number of separate legal instruments of intellectual property, particularly protecting both the utilitarian aspects (through utility patent) and aesthetic features (through copyright, design patent, or trade dress) of the vessel hull. At the same time, if a design patent is issued for a vessel hull design protected under the VHDPA, the latter protection shall terminate simultaneously (Section 1229).

However, according to the Copyright Office, only a couple of dozens of vessel design registrations were made every year from 1998 to 2012. In 2013, only two vessel designs were registered, and there have been no registrations since then.[74] Although the VHDPA still remains effective, absence of any design registration in the past 10-year period demonstrates that the experience with the *sui generis* regime for vessel hull designs can hardly be called a success. This, in turn, casts doubt upon whether a *sui generis* legal regime for other kinds of designs can be successful as well.

In particular, there have been a number of attempts to introduce *sui generis* protection for fashion designs. Three bills named Design Piracy Prohibition Act were introduced in Congress in 2007 and 2010, proposing to extend copyright protection to clothing, handbags, and eyeglasses frames.[75] None of the bills eventually became law. As an alternative to the DPPA, the Innovative Design Protection and Piracy Prevention Act (IDPPPA)[76] was proposed in 2011, and its revised version, the Innovative Design Protection Act,[77] followed in 2012.

All of these bills proposed to extend the scope of Chapter 13 "Protection of Original Designs" of Title 17 of the U.S. Code to fashion designs. Thus, the bills specifically named fashion designs as protected designs, same as "vessel features" (Section 1301(a)), and proposed to amend the definition of "useful article" by adding articles of apparel. The bills define fashion design as the appearance as a whole of an article of apparel and the original elements of the article of apparel or the original arrangement or placement of original or non-original elements. The IDPPPA and IDPA specified that such elements or arrangement should be the result of a designer's own creative endeavor and provide a unique, distinguishable, non-trivial, and non-utilitarian variation over prior designs for similar types of articles. All the bills proposed a term of protection of three years, which is much shorter than that afforded to vessel hull designs, lasting ten years. The DPPA stated that a design is not infringing if it is original and not closely and substantially similar in overall visual

[73] Bradley J. Olson, 'The Vessel Hull Design Protection Act of 1998: is it still afloat?' (n 68) citing Prof. William Fryer, Vessel Hull Design Protection Act: Hearing on HR 2696 Before the House Subcommittee on Courts and Intellectual Property. 105 Cong. 28 (1997).

[74] U.S. Copyright Office. Vessel Design Registration <https://www.copyright.gov/vessels/list/> accessed 4 September 2022.

[75] Congress. Design Privacy Prohibition Acts S.1957—110th Congress (2007–2008), H.R.2033—110th Congress (2007–2008), H.R.2196—111th Congress (2009–2010).

[76] H.R.2511—112th Congress (2011–2012).

[77] S.3523—112th Congress (2011–2012).

appearance to a protected design, if it merely reflects a trend, or if it is the result of independent creation.

However, each time these bills were proposed, they met strong opposition from different lobbying groups. Interestingly, one of the main opponents of the DPPA was American Apparel and Footwear Association, arguing that "the Copyright Office would never be able to handle the flood of applications; the proposed protection standard was not sufficiently well defined; and the standard for infringement was too vague, so that the courts would spend years trying to define it, rather than enforcing it".[78]

The critics of the IDPPPA pointed out that design protection legislation would just raise the costs of doing business in the fashion industry and keep young designers from entering into the fashion industry because of a fear of litigation.[79] There were particular concerns as to the definition of "substantially identical" fashion design, meaning "an article of apparel which is so similar in appearance as to be likely to be mistaken for the protected design, and contains only those differences in construction or design which are merely trivial" (Section 3.2(a)). It was unclear who would be deciding on this standard—an average person, some percentage of the population, or a fashion expert. But in any case, this would lead to unpredictable and inconsistent verdicts, which means that the IDPPPA would benefit neither designers nor consumers, but lawyers.[80]

As to the argument that the U.S. should implement similar design protection legislation as in the E.U., Sprigman, the co-author of the well-known work on the piracy paradox in the fashion industry,[81] notes that, in his view, the European experience has been mostly negative, as design laws are not used a lot and copying still takes place in the E.U. Besides, such law could even be harmful in the U.S., since the U.S. has a stronger civil litigation system, and thus the fashion industry's attention might be turned away from innovation towards litigation.[82]

---

[78] Louis S. Ederer, Maxwell Preston, 'The Innovation Design Protection and Piracy Prevention Act—Fashion Industry Friend or Faux?' (2011) LexisNexis Communities Copyright and Trademark Law <https://www.lexisnexis.com/legalnewsroom/intellectual-property/b/copyright-trademark-law-blog/posts/the-innovative-design-protection-and-piracy-prevention-act-fashion-industry-friend-or-faux> accessed 9 September 2022.

[79] Lauren E. Purcell, 'A Fashion Flop: the Innovative Design Protection and Piracy Prevention Act' (2012–2013) 31 Journal of Law & Commerce 207, 221–224.

[80] Innovative Design Protection and Privacy Prevention Act. Hearing before the Subcommittee on Intellectual Property, Competition, and the Internet of the Committee of the Judiciary House of Representatives 112th Congress, first session on H.R. 2511, July 15, 2011. Serial No. 112–46. Testimony of Christopher Sprigman, Professor of Law, University of Virginia School of Law <https://www.govinfo.gov/content/pkg/CHRG-112hhrg67397/pdf/CHRG-112hhrg67397.pdf> accessed 7 September 2022.

[81] Kal Raustiala and Christopher Sprigman, 'The Piracy Paradox: Innovation and Intellectual Property in Fashion Design' (2006) 92 Virginia Law Review 1687.

[82] Innovative Design Protection and Privacy Prevention Act. Hearing before the Subcommittee on Intellectual Property, Competition, and the Internet of the Committee of the Judiciary House of Representatives 112th Congress, first session on H.R. 2511, July 15, 2011.Serial No. 112–46.

At the same time, other authors praise the EU approach noting that it has had a well-grounded design protection system for years, with the winning weapon being the protection for unregistered designs.[83]

A number of scholars believe that *sui generis* protection, not necessarily similar to the one in the EU, is still needed for certain kinds of designs, particularly for fashion designs possessing "exceptional originality".[84] Jimenez proposes that *sui generis* protection should possess a higher standard of originality than copyright, asserting that "the fashion design is the result of a designer's own creative endeavor and provides a unique, distinguishable, nontrivial and non-utilitarian variation over prior designs for similar types of articles". Along with the high standard of originality, a high standard of infringement, Jimenez claims, is also crucial for fashion designs. The proposed "substantially identical" standard for infringement "would allow adaptations of trend features, but would prohibit close copying of differentiating features, such that one article could be mistaken for the other". In the view of Jimenez, this is one of the reasons why *sui generis* protection is the appropriate form of protection for fashion designs—because, "while in other creative fields close imitations are considered harmful", in the fashion industry "it is these commonalities in creative elements that drive it and spur further creation".

In sum, although copyright, design patent, and trademark law remain available for the protection of designs in the U.S., a significant percentage of designs remain unprotected. Taking into consideration the limited positive impact of the vessel hull design protection, as well as the opinions of a large number of scholars and practitioners opposing a *sui generis* design regime, it is unlikely that another *sui generis* design law could be introduced in the U.S. in the near future.

3.3 Conclusions

Thus, the *sui generis* regime for the legal protection of designs has been introduced in both the U.S. and the EU. However, these two kinds of experiences on both sides of the Atlantic differ significantly.

The U.S. has introduced the *sui generis* regime exclusively for vessel hull designs, after strong lobbying following the Supreme Court's decision in *Bonito Boats Inc. v. Thunder Craft Boats Inc.* However, this *sui generis* right turned out to be hardly used in the industry, with no applications filed in the past ten years. This experience cast

---

Testimony of Christopher Sprigman, Professor of Law, University of Virginia School of Law (n 80).

[83] Silvia Beltrametti, 'Evaluation of the Design Piracy Prohibition Act: Is the Cure Worse than the Disease? An Analogy with Counterfeiting and a Comparison with the Protection Available in the European Community' (2010) 8 Northwestern Journal of Technology and Intellectual Property 147, 148.

[84] Arianne Vanessa Josephine T. Jimenez, 'A Sui Generis System of Protection for Exceptionally Original Fashion Designs'(2016) 36 Loyola of Los Angeles Entertainment Law Review 101.

reasonable doubts as to whether the extension of the *sui generis* intellectual property protection to any other kind of design would have a positive outcome.

The EU, after the enactment of the Design Directive aimed at harmonization of national substantive registered design law, introduced the Community Designs—a *sui generis* regime providing an anti-copying right for unregistered designs and an exclusive right for registered designs. Same as with the *sui generis* regime for the legal protection of databases, the primary objective of the special design regime was to harmonize national design laws and promote a single market for products embodying design. The most recent evaluation of the design protection legislation in the EU has proved the effectiveness of the design regime, which is also affirmed by the growing number of applications for RCDs, significantly exceeding the numbers of design patent applications in the U.S.

The reasons for the difference in these kinds of experience with a *sui generis* regime for designs in the U.S. and the EU lie in the differences between the *sui generis* rights. First, the *sui generis* regime in the U.S. was introduced for just one of multiple design industries. Second, the effectiveness of a legal regime is judged by its objectives. So far, the examples of databases and designs have demonstrated that a *sui generis* intellectual property regime effectively accomplishes the purpose of harmonizing national laws and facilitating a single market.

Chapter 4
Sui Generis Intellectual Property Protection for Plant Varieties

Plant breeding means application of genetic principles to produce plants that are more useful to humans.[1] Traditionally, the breeding methods for creation of new plant varieties included the selection and crossing of individual plants with improved traits. Nowadays, a new plant variety can be created by either traditional breeding methods or with genetic engineering.[2] "Experiments on Plant Hybridization" ("*Versuche über Pflanzen-Hybriden*") was the first work on plant breeding and genetics made by an Augustinian monk Gregor Mendel, who experimented with pea plant (*Pisum sativum*) breeding and discovered the principles of inheritance.[3]

Planting material has long been regarded as a highly valued communal and public resource. With the growth of the population, as well as with industrialization, the interest in plant breeding has been constantly increasing. For these reasons, plant breeding is widely supported in many jurisdictions by an array of economic and legal incentives, including prizes, public investment, tax benefits, and intellectual property rights.[4] In addition, the availability of intellectual property protection instruments for plant varieties is considered to have an impact on the amount of investments into the plant breeding industry.

Among the intellectual property rights, the following instruments are available for the protection of plant varieties: patents, trade secret, and a *sui generis* system.

---

[1] Britannica. Plant breeding <https://www.britannica.com/science/plant-breeding> accessed 13 October 2022.

[2] Barbara Fleck and Claire Baldock, 'Intellectual property protection for plant-related inventions in Europe' (2003) 4 Nature Reviews Genetics 834.

[3] Ilona Miko, 'Gregor Mendel and the principles of inheritance' (2008) 1(1) Nature Education 134 <https://www.nature.com/scitable/topicpage/gregor-mendel-and-the-principles-of-inheritance-593/> accessed 13 October 2022.

[4] Niels Louwaars and Jan Engels, 'Intellectual property rights: patents or sui generis systems?' in Conny Almekinders and Walter de Boef (eds), *Encouraging diversity. The conservation and development of plant genetic resources* (Intermediate Technology Publications 2000) 279.

I. Kazeeva, *Sui Generis Intellectual Property Protection*, Perspectives in Law, Business and Innovation, https://doi.org/10.1007/978-981-99-8897-6_4

Patents can be applied for the protection of plant varieties in the U.S. However, in many countries, plant varieties are typically not eligible for patent protection. Article 27(3) of the TRIPS Agreement authorizes member states to exclude from patentability plants, animals, and essentially biological processes for the production of plants or animals. Louwaars and Engels name three categories of the reasons why most countries do not grant patent protection to plant varieties: (1) ethical, since patenting forms of life is considered unethical, (2) technical, due to self-replicating nature and lack of inventive component in the subject matter, and (3) economic reasons, due to the importance of the subject matter for the food and nutrition state policies. A very strong instrument of protection, patents would limit the freedom of both farmers and other breeders and potentially lock complete gene pools, leading to monopolistic situations.[5]

Trade secrets are generally used to protect devices, strategies, or other information that is a competitive advantage.[6] In particular, trade secret may be used in order to protect the parental plant lines of hybrid seeds, i.e., seeds produced by crossing plants belonging to different varieties, as opposed to self-pollinated crops. At the same time, the enforceability of such trade secrets remains questionable since trade secret status requires taking precautions in order to maintain secrecy, whereas the parental lines are often planted over wide areas.[7] However, in *Pioneer Hi-Bred Intern. v. Holden Foundation Seeds, Inc.*, the Court of Appeals affirmed that plant parental lines (genetic messages) can qualify for trade secret status.[8] Another issue making trade secret protection for hybrid seeds questionable is the probability that in a large quantity of hybrid seed there will be an occasional seed that was self-pollinated by the maternal plant, thus revealing the parental line.[9]

The ISF provides other examples of information that can be protected as trade secrets in the field of plant breeding and biotechnology: breeding records, specific methods that are used in the laboratory, workshop, greenhouse or field, molecular markers used in marker assisted selection.[10]

Sui generis protection for plant varieties is facilitated by international agreements. In 1957, the twelve European countries were participating in the International Association of Plant Breeders for the Protection of Plant Varieties (ASSINSEL)[11] Conference discussing the protection of new plant varieties. One of the main questions on

[5] Ibid 280.

[6] International Seed Federation. A Guide to Intellectual Property <https://worldseed.org/wp-content/uploads/2021/05/IP-Guide-v15-31may2021.pdf> accessed 4 October 2022.

[7] Nicholas S. Seay, 'Intellectual Property in Plants' in P. Stephen Baenziger, Roger A. Kleese, Robert F Barnes (eds), *Intellectual Property Rights: Protection of Plant Materials* 61, 66 (Crop Science Society of America 1993).

[8] *Pioneer Hi-Bred International v. Holden Foundation Seeds, Inc.*, 35 F.3d 1226 (1994).

[9] Nicholas S. Seay, 'Intellectual Property in Plants' (n 7) 66.

[10] International Seed Federation. ISF View on Intellectual Property, adopted in Rio de Janeiro, Brazil, 28 June 2012 <https://worldseed.org/wp-content/uploads/2015/10/View_on_Intellectual_Property_2012.pdf> accessed 21 December 2022.

[11] In 2002, ASSINSEL and International Seed Trade Federation (FIS) merged to become the International Seed Federation (ISF).

the agenda was to decide between revising national patent laws and creating a new plant breeder's right. It was finally decided in favor of a specifically designed *sui generis* right, for the following reasons: (1) plants could not meet the patent law requirement of novelty, (2) plant breeding processes could rarely be shown to be inventive, (3) it would not be in the public interest to allow plant breeders to have a monopoly over plant varieties, (4) it is difficult to meet the patent law disclosure requirement, as following the description of plant breeding could not guarantee the same result because of possible mutations.[12]

The International Union for the Protection of New Varieties of Plants (UPOV), an independent intergovernmental body established in 1961 and including 78 member countries, provides for a *sui generis* form of intellectual property protection of plant varieties in order to encourage the breeders in creating new varieties of plants.[13] In UPOV terms, a "variety" means a plant grouping within a single botanical taxon of the lowest known rank, which grouping can be (1) defined by the expression of the characteristics resulting from a given genotype or combination of genotypes, (2) distinguished from any other plant grouping by the expression of at least one of the said characteristics, and (3) considered as a unit with regard to its suitability for being propagated unchanged (Article 1 of the UPOV Convention).[14] Thus, a plant variety is a precisely defined group of plants, selected from within a species, with a common set of characteristics.[15] Under the UPOV Convention, granting and protecting breeders' rights is the basic obligation of the contracting parties (Article 2).

One of the key distinctions of a *sui generis* regime as compared to patents is that a patent provides protection to all variants of plant varieties falling within the scope of the invention, whereas a *sui generis* regime refers to a particular plant variety.[16] This is because the breeder's right provides the rightholder with control over the propagating material of the protected variety (Article 14 of the UPOV Convention), whereas patents grant exclusive rights for an invention, that can be not only a product, but also a process. Besides, the important characteristics of the UPOV *sui generis* model, as compared to patents, are the requirements for novelty, distinctiveness, uniformity, and stability, as well as the exceptions to the breeder's right. A breeder's right is granted where the variety is new (meaning, the propagating or harvested material of the variety has not been sold or otherwise disposed of to others for purposes of exploitation); distinct (it is clearly distinguishable from any other variety whose existence is a matter of common knowledge at the time of the filing of the application); uniform (meaning sufficiently uniform in its relevant characteristics);

[12] Margaret Llewelyn and Mike Adcock 'European plant intellectual property' (Oxford: Hart Publishing 2006).

[13] UPOV <https://www.upov.int/about/en/> accessed 1 October 2022.

[14] International Convention for the Protection of New Varieties of Plants of December 2, 1961, as Revised at Geneva on November 10, 1972, on October 23, 1978, and on March 19, 1991 <https://www.upov.int/edocs/pubdocs/en/upov_pub_221.pdf> accessed 21 December 2022.

[15] UPOV. What is a plant variety? <https://www.upov.int/overview/en/variety.html#varieties> accessed 21 December 2022.

[16] Barbara Fleck and Claire Baldock, 'Intellectual property protection for plant-related inventions in Europe' (n 2).

and stable (meaning its relevant characteristics remain unchanged after repeated propagation or at the end of each cycle of propagation) (Articles 5–9). With regard to varieties protected by a breeder's right, production, offering for sale, marketing, exporting, and importing of the propagating material of the protected variety shall require prior authorization of the breeder (Article 14). The period of protection shall be not less than 20 years from the date of the grant of the breeder's right, whereas, for trees and vines, the minimum period of protection is 25 years (Article 19).

Exceptions to the breeder's right include acts done privately and for non-commercial purposes, for experimental purposes, as well as acts done for the purpose of breeding other varieties (breeder's exemption) (Article 15). Thus, the breeder's exemption allows other breeders to freely use important genetic material for breeding of other plant varieties. An optional exception from breeders' rights that member countries can introduce into their legislation is allowing farmers to use for propagating purposes the product of the harvest which they have obtained by planting the protected variety (farmer's privilege). Such non-commercial use is limited to the holdings of the farmer and only "within reasonable limits and subject to the safeguarding of the legitimate interests of the breeder". This provision, for instance, allows farmers in developing countries to use seeds of protected plant varieties for their own food supply.

Notably, before the 1991 revision of the UPOV Convention, Article 2 "Forms of protection" allowed member states to protect plant varieties by a patent system, but prohibited application of both patent and *sui generis* forms of protection for the same botanical genus or species. This prohibition was removed with the 1991 Act of the UPOV Convention.[17]

An obligation to protect plant varieties also exists for all WTO members. Under Article 27(3) of the TRIPS Agreement, member states should "provide for the protection of plant varieties either by patents or by an effective *sui generis* system or by any combination thereof". However, the TRIPS Agreement does not define what constitutes an "effective" *sui generis* system, so the member countries can choose the plant varieties protection system that suits their interests best. Thus, all WTO members are bound to protect plant varieties, but there is flexibility as to the particular form of protection.[18] The UPOV breeders' rights regime is one of the models that meets the requirements of Article 27(3) of the TRIPS Agreement.

Being members of both the TRIPS Agreement and the UPOV Convention, the EU and the U.S. have implemented their own plant varieties protection systems, which, however, differ significantly and can be used simultaneously with other instruments of legal protection.

---

[17] 1991 Act of the UPOV Convention <https://upovlex.upov.int/en/convention> accessed 9 October 2022.

[18] Carlos M. Correa, 'Sui generis protection for farmers' varieties' in Michael Halewood (ed) Farmers' Crop Varieties and Farmers' Rights. Challenges in Taxonomy and Law (Routledge 2016).

4.1 Legal Protection of Plant Varieties in the EU

In 1949, at the first meeting of the Consultative Assembly of the Council of Europe, the question of creating a European Patent Office was discussed. Shortly thereafter, the Committee of Ministers established the Committee of Experts on Patents of the Council of Europe, comprised of the national highest officials in charge of the national patent services.[19]

In 1960, in light of the discussions on the *sui generis* system of the UPOV Convention, the Council issued a statement saying that harmonizing national law provisions of patentability of plant varieties would be too difficult and that a *sui generis* form of protection was more suitable for plant varieties than patents.[20]

The work of the Council further resulted in the Convention on the Unification of Certain Points of Substantive Law on Patents for Invention signed in Strasbourg in 1963[21] and the European Patent Convention signed in Munich in 1973.[22]

The EPC, being separate from the EU, has 39 signatories, including all EU Member States and 12 states not being members of the EU. The European Patent Office grants a European patent which results in a bundle of national patents valid in the designated EPC contracting states (Article 79 EPC), thus saving costs of parallel national applications. Under the EPC, European patents shall not be granted to "plant or animal varieties or essentially biological processes for the production of plants or animals", with the exception of microbiological processes or the products thereof (Article 53(b)).

In the 1990s, with the development of genetic engineering and little guidance from patent law, the EPO found itself in untested waters. The early decisions of the EPO on cases relating to genetic modifications in plants "created more confusion than useful guidelines as to how GMOs might be protected by patents in Europe".[23]

In order to provide clarity on what biotechnological inventions, including plant varieties, should be patentable, as well as to harmonize the laws of the Member States, in 1998 the EU adopted a Directive on the legal protection of biotechnological inventions.[24] In the Explanatory Statement to the 1997 Report on the Proposal for the Directive, it was particularly noted that, given the divergences between the European and national patent systems, it was appropriate to seek practical conformity between the EPC, and national patent laws. Therefore, approximating the national patent laws

---

[19] Per Von Holstein, 'International Co-operation in the Field of Patent Law with Special Reference to the Activities of the Council of Europe' (1967) 16/1 The International and Comparative Law Quarterly 191.

[20] Margaret Llewelyn and Mike Adcock 'European plant intellectual property' (n 12).

[21] Council of Europe. Convention on the Unification of Certain Points of Substantive Law on Patents for Invention <https://rm.coe.int/168006b65d> accessed 15 October 2022.

[22] European Patent Office. The European Patent Convention <https://www.epo.org/law-practice/legal-texts/html/epc/2016/e/ar53.html> accessed 2 October 2022.

[23] Barbara Fleck and Claire Baldock, 'Intellectual property protection for plant-related inventions in Europe' (n 2) 835.

[24] Directive 98/44/EC of the European Parliament and of the Council of 6 July 1998 on the legal protection of biotechnological inventions [1998] OJ L213/13.

in the field of biotechnology was one of the main objectives of the Directive, with the EPO being "expected to take this development into account in its practices".[25]

The Directive requires all Member States to protect biotechnological inventions under national patent law (Article 1). Biotechnological inventions shall be patentable if they are new, involve an inventing step, and are susceptible of industrial application (Article 3). However, Article 4 provides that plant and animal varieties, as well as essentially biological processes for the production of plants or animals, are not patentable ("essentially biological process" meaning the process of production of plants or animals consisting entirely of natural phenomena, such as crossing or selection (Article 2)). Also, plant- or animal-related inventions are patentable "if the technical feasibility of the invention is not confined to a particular plant or animal variety". Unpatentable are also those inventions, the commercial exploitation of which would be contrary to *ordre public* or morality. However, exploitation shall not be deemed to be contrary to *ordre public* merely because it is prohibited by law or regulation (Article 6).

In order to avoid a situation when a breeder cannot exploit a plant variety right because the biotechnological invention is protected by a patent, Article 12 provides for compulsory licenses for non-exclusive use of the invention that the patent holder should grant to the breeder, subject to payment of an appropriate royalty. The same principle applies for the other way round situations, where a holder of a patent for a biotechnological invention cannot exploit it without infringing a prior plant variety right, thus the compulsory license for the non-exclusive use of the plant variety is granted to the patent holder, subject to payment of an appropriate royalty.

In the same year of the adoption of the Directive on the Legal Protection of Biotechnological Inventions, the Netherlands, supported by Italy and Norway, brought Case C-377/98[26] before the CJEU for the annulment of the Directive. Among other pleas, the applicant alleged that the obligations imposed on the Member States by the Directive were incompatible with the obligations resulting from a number of international undertakings, namely, the TRIPS Agreement, the Agreement on Technical Barriers to Trade, the EPC, and the Convention on Biological Diversity signed on 5 June 1992 in Rio de Janeiro. In particular, the Netherlands argued that, while Article 27(3)(b) of the TRIPS Agreement allows not to grant a patent for plants and animals other than micro-organisms, the Directive deprives Member States of such choice. However, the ECJ rejected the pleas of the applicant, stating that the option taken in Article 4 of the Directive is in itself compatible with the TRIPS Agreement and "the joint selection of an option offered by an international instrument to which the Member States are parties is an act that falls within the approximation of laws provided for by

[25] Report on the proposal for a European Parliament and Council Directive on the legal protection of biotechnological inventions (COM (95)0661-C4-0063/96-95/0350(COD)), Rapporteur: Mr Willi Rothley, 25 June 1997, p. 32 <https://www.europarl.europa.eu/doceo/document/A-4-1997-0222_EN.pdf?redirect> accessed 14 October 2022.

[26] Case C-377/98 *Kingdom of the Netherlands v European Parliament and Council of the European Union* [2001] ECR I-07079.

Article 100a of the Treaty" (now, Article 95 of the Treaty establishing the European Community[27]) (para. 58).

One of the most important cases shaping the European Patent Office's practice, decided in the time of enactment of the Directive on the Legal Protection of Biotechnological inventions, has been the *Novartis* case.[28] The case started with the rejection of a patent application with the title "Anti-pathogenically effective compositions comprising lytic peptides and hydrolytic enzymes", referring to "a transgenic plant and the seed thereof" comprising certain recombinant DNA sequences, as well as methods of preparing such transgenic plants. The Examining Division refused the application holding that "a claim to genetically engineered plants and seeds, although not directed to any specific plant varieties, encompassed plant varieties which were not products of a microbiological process and, consequently, was not allowed under Article 53(b) EPC". Novartis disagreed arguing that Article 53(b) was inappropriately interpreted and the patent should be granted. There was a number of key decisions on the case: one by the Technical Board of Appeal published in October 1997 and another by the Enlarged Board of Appeal taken in December 1999. In between these decisions, the Directive on the legal protection of biotechnological inventions was enacted—the fact which presumably influenced the reasoning of the EPO. In its final decision, the Enlarged Board of Appeal held that the intention of the draftsmen of the EPC was not to ban protection of all types of plant material, but rather to exclude those plant groupings that were protectable under the UPOV Convention, so as to avoid simultaneous double protection. This was also in line with the statement of the Community Plant Variety Office, saying that it preferred an approach where a claim covering a plant variety would be rejected. Thus, the Enlarged Board of Appeal overruled nearly all arguments of the Technical Board of Appeal and cemented the EPO practice for the following years.After the *Novartis* decision, Article 53(b) EPC applied only to plant groupings that were protected under the plant varieties rights, while all other plant material was patentable. As to claims to plant groupings encompassing plant varieties, they were patentable, provided that the claims were not specifically directed to an individual plant variety.[29]

More recent landmark decisions affecting the practice of the EPO are the decisions in cases G2/12 and G2/13 concerning the patentability of a reduced water content wrinkly tomato and a broccoli variety which could reduce the risk of getting cancer. In 2015, the Enlarged Board of Appeal held in these cases that plants derived from essentially biological processes were patentable.

However, in 2016, the Commission issued a Notice stating that the patentability of products derived from using essentially biological processes that was confirmed in the decisions of the Enlarged Board of Appeal "runs into potential conflict with the legal protection provided to plant varieties under EU plant variety legislation as

---

[27] Treaty establishing the European Community (Consolidated version 2002) [2002] OJ C 325.

[28] T1054/96 'Plants/NOVARTIS' [1998] OJ EPO 511.

[29] Margaret Llewelyn and Mike Adcock 'European plant intellectual property' (n 12).

regards access to genetic resources".[30] In particular, the Commission observed that certain provisions of the Directive indicate that the EU legislator's intention when adopting the Directive was to exclude from patentability products that are obtained by means of essentially biological processes. For instance, Recital 32 states that "if an invention consists only in genetically modifying a particular plant variety, and if a new plant variety is bred, it will still be excluded from patentability even if the genetic modification is the result *not of an essentially biological process* but of a biotechnological process" (italicized in the Commission Notice). The trigger point for ensuring the patentability of a plant, the Commission noted, is the technical process (e.g., inserting a gene into a genome), whereas "essentially biological processes are not of a technical nature and therefore, according to the position taken by the legislator, they cannot be covered by a patent".

In 2017, the new Rule 28(2) was enacted, stating that "European patents shall not be granted in respect of plants or animals exclusively obtained by means of an essentially biological process".[31] This led the Enlarged Board of Appeal to overturn the decisions in cases G2/12 and G2/13. In order to provide legal certainty for patent proprietors, the new interpretation of Article 53(b) was decided to have no retroactive effect on European patents granted before 1 July 2017.[32] However, some scholars note that the new Rule 28(2) just fixed the initial intention of the EU legislator in written form, as in fact it never intended to allow patents on plants and animals derived from essentially biological processes.[33]

As the *sui generis* protection system for plant varieties was discussed on the international level, the EU set plans for introducing a Community-wide plant breeding right.

Historically, one of the first initiatives to grant special legal protection to plant varieties among the European countries was undertaken in France. In 1883, an unsuccessful attempt was made to introduce a special plant protection law. At the Congress of the Pomological Society in 1904, the fruit breeders requested for a system of registration of new plant varieties, as well as for creating a certificate that would grant an exclusive right to propagate the new variety for a limited period of time. In 1922, a variety register was created. Ten years later, a new catalogue for cultivated plant varieties was introduced, where all new varieties had to be entered before being put into commerce. In 1934, Germany enacted specific plant protection legislation,

---

[30] Commission Notice on certain articles of Directive 98/44/EC of the European Parliament and of the Council on the legal protection of biotechnological inventions C/2016/6997 [2016] OJ C 411/3.

[31] European Patent Office. The European Patent Convention. Rule 28. Exceptions to patentability <https://www.epo.org/law-practice/legal-texts/html/epc/2016/e/r28.html> accessed 2 October 2022.

[32] European Patent Office. Press Communiqué of 14 May 2020 concerning opinion G 3/19 of the Enlarged Board of Appeal <https://www.epo.org/law-practice/case-law-appeals/communications/2020/20200514.html> accessed 2 October 2022.

[33] 'Correct legal interpretation of Article 53(b), EPC, regarding the patentability of essentially biological processes in relation to plants and animals within the context of the EU patent directive 98/44' (No Patents on Seeds! 2021) <https://www.no-patents-on-seeds.org/sites/default/files/news/Correct%20interpretation%20of%20Art.%2053(b).pdf> accessed 14 October 2022.

permitting patents for plants at the same time.[34] The Netherlands also established a system for protection of new plant varieties in the 1940s. However, until the end of the twentieth century, most European countries did not have special intellectual property protection for new varieties of plants.[35]

The first draft of the legal act that would introduce a Community-wide plant breeding right was prepared in 1990. However, the consultations on the draft were postponed in order to await the results of the 1991 Diplomatic Conference for the revision of the UPOV Convention.[36] After the 1991 Act of the UPOV Convention was adopted, the draft was amended accordingly. The final text of the Regulation on Community plant variety rights[37] was adopted in 1994. More than 10 years later, in 2005, the European Community acceded to the UPOV Convention,[38] thus being the first supranational organization to become an UPOV member.[39]

The EU system of Community plant variety rights is an intellectual property right similar to patents, protecting new plant varieties and effective throughout the EU. The protectable subject matter of the CPVR are varieties of all botanical genera and species, including hybrids between genera or species (Article 5 of the Regulation on Community plant variety rights). The conditions of protection are in line with the requirements under the UPOV model; in particular, a variety must be distinct, uniform, stable, and new (Articles 6–10). The breeder entitled to the CPVR is the person who bred, or discovered and developed the variety, or his successor in title. In case the breeder is an employee, the entitlement of the CPVR shall be determined in accordance with the applicable national employment law (Article 11). Under the CPVR, the production or reproduction, offering for sale, selling, exporting, importing, stocking of the protected variety shall require authorization of the CPVR holder (Article 13). The Regulation on CPVR also includes the three exceptions to the breeder's right stipulated in the UPOV Convention (Article 15), as well as the optional farmer's privilege (Article 14(1)). The CPVR shall run until the end of the 25th calendar year following the year of the grant, whereas for vine and tree species the term of protection is until the end of the 30th calendar year (Article 19).

Interestingly, unlike other instruments of intellectual property rights, such as copyright, patent, and trademarks, the CPVR system coexists with the national systems for protection of plant varieties based on the UPOV Convention. In particular, the

---

[34] Margaret Llewelyn and Mike Adcock 'European plant intellectual property' (n 12).

[35] Gert Würtenberger, Martin Ekvad, Paul van der Kooij, Bart Kiewiet, 'European Union Plant Variety Protection' (Oxford University Press 2021).

[36] UPOV Press Release No. 8 'Diplomatic Conference for the revision of the International Convention for the Protection of New Varieties of Plants' Geneva, 21 March 1991 <https://www.upov.int/edocs/pressdocs/en/upov_pr_008.pdf> accessed 13 October 2022.

[37] Council Regulation (EC) 2100/94 of 27 July 1994 on Community plant variety rights [1994] OJ L227/1.

[38] Council Decision of 30 May 2005, approving the accession of the European Community to the International Convention for the Protection of New Varieties of Plants, as revised in Geneva on 19 March 1991 [2005] OJ L192.

[39] Gert Würtenberger, Martin Ekvad, Paul van der Kooij, Bart Kiewiet, 'European Union Plant Variety Protection' (n 35).

Regulation prohibits cumulative protection by both national regime and CPVR. Thus, in case CPVR is granted for a variety protected by a national right or patent, the latter will be rendered ineffective for the term of the CPVR (Article 92). So, the CPVR system "neither substitutes nor harmonizes such national systems, but is thought to be an alternative to them".[40] However, it is noted that there have been no discrepancies as to the scope of the CPVR and national rights, as both of them use the same UPOV standards and UPOV test guidelines.[41]

Over the period from the creation of the CPVR in 1995, the number of titles for the CPVR granted to breeders has been relatively stable each year, being below 2,000 titles granted annually before 2004 and over 2,000 titles starting from 2004.[42] In 2021, 2,859 titles for the CPVR were granted (against 3,480 applications received), which was a drop of 4% compared to 2020, that was the third highest in 25 years. The overall number of titles for the CPVR in 2022 is approximately 30,000.[43]

According to the evaluation of the CPVR conducted by the Commission in 2011, the CPVR system provides uniform, harmonized EU-wide intellectual property protection for new plant varieties, incentivizing breeders to invest in research and develop new plant varieties. The evaluation particularly noted the breeder's exception, being the most important feature of the CPVR system, facilitating innovation and encouraging competition in the breeding industry. The evaluation also pointed out a number of weaknesses to be addressed. Namely, although the CPVR system provides for a harmonized intellectual property regime for plant varieties at EU level, enforcement varies widely in practice across the Member States. The Commission also noted the overlap with the EU legislative framework for patents, absence of effective royalty collection arrangements for farm-saved seeds in the Member States, etc. Despite the mentioned weaknesses, the Commission concluded that the CPVR system "functions well and has met its objectives".[44]

Thus, with plant varieties being excluded from patent protection, which was confirmed by the latest EPO decisions, the EU created a Community-wide plant variety rights system, thus facilitating the single market for plant varieties. However, the plant variety rights were not as successful in the U.S., which urged making patent protection available for plants.

---

[40] Ibid.

[41] Ibid.

[42] CPVO. EU Plant Variety Rights. Some Figures < https://food.ec.europa.eu/system/files/2019-12/plant_variety_conf_20111011_cpvo.pdf> accessed 5 October 2022 (EU Plant Variety Rights in the twenty-first century conference—October 2011).

[43] CPVO. Annual Report 2021 <https://cpvo.europa.eu/sites/default/files/documents/20220571_pdf_tgac22001enn_002_vc.pdf> accessed 5 October 2022.

[44] European Commission. Food safety. Plant variety property rights. Evaluation <https://food.ec.europa.eu/plants/plant-variety-property-rights/evaluation_en> accessed 5 October 2022.

4.2 Legal Protection of Plant Varieties in the U.S.

In the U.S., a special patent instrument for plants was enacted as early as 1930. The Plant Patent Act provided that a patent be granted to "whoever invents or discovers and asexually reproduces any distinct and new variety of plant, including cultivated sports, mutants, hybrids, and newly found seedlings, other than a tuber propagated plant or a plant found in an uncultivated state".[45] The purpose of the bill, according to an Indiana Representative Purnell, was to "afford agriculture, so far as is practicable, the same opportunity to participate in the benefits of the patent system as have been given industry".[46] The grant lasts for 20 years from the date of filing of the application and allows the patent owner to exclude others from asexually reproducing the plant, using, offering for sale, selling, or importing the plant (Section 163). The plant patent must satisfy the general requirements of patentability, except that the requirements to the written description of the invention specified in Section 112 do not apply to plant patents, provided that "the description is as complete as is reasonably possible" (Section 162). According to the USPTO, the number of granted plant patents has been steadily growing over the years, with only 129 plant patents granted in 1963 and more than a thousand plant patents granted each year starting from 2014.[47]

However, many breeders were not able to acquire protection under the PPA for their varieties, in particular because it was difficult to meet the threshold for protection.[48]

The creation of UPOV in 1961, as well as the advancement of technology of plant breeding facilitated the enactment of the Plant Variety Protection Act in 1970.[49] The PVPA provides legal intellectual property rights protection to breeders of new varieties of plants that are sexually reproduced (by seed) or tuber-propagated.[50] Varieties are protected if they are novel and possess distinctiveness (meaning, they are clearly distinguishable from any other variety the existence of which is publicly known), uniformity (any variations are describable, predictable, and commercially acceptable), and stability (the variety, when reproduced, will remain unchanged with regard to the essential and distinctive characteristics of the variety).[51] The certificates granted by the Plant Variety Protection Office protect varieties for 20 years (25 years

---

[45] 35 U.S.C. Ch. 15 Section 161.

[46] United States House of Representatives. History, Art & Archives. Historical Highlights. Plant Patent Act of 1930 <https://history.house.gov/Historical-Highlights/1901-1950/1930_05_13_Plant_Patent/> accessed 3 October 2022.

[47] U.S. Patent and Trademark Office. Patent Technology Monitoring Team (PTMT). U.S. Patent Statistics Char. Calendar Years 1963–2020 <https://www.uspto.gov/web/offices/ac/ido/oeip/taf/us_stat.htm> accessed 3 October 2022.

[48] Margaret Llewelyn and Mike Adcock 'European plant intellectual property' (n 12) 80.

[49] 7 U.S.C. §§ 2321–2582.

[50] U.S. Department of Agriculture. Plant Variety Protection Act <https://www.ams.usda.gov/rules-regulations/pvpa> accessed 3 October 2022.

[51] 7 U.S.C. § 2402.

for vines and trees), are recognized worldwide, and allow their owners to exclude others from marketing and selling their varieties.[52]

In contrast to the European model, the plant material is generally not examined by the PVPO, unless there is a query from a third party claiming that the plant material does not meet the protection requirements. For these reasons, the U.S. plant variety protection system is considered to be a right by registration and, therefore, weaker than the systems provided by other UPOV members, as the granted right may be subject to challenge.[53]

As observed by some scholars, the rights granted under the PVPA were "ostensibly in line with the principles of the UPOV Convention".[54] As noted above, the 1991 Act of the UPOV Convention removed the prohibition of applying both patent and *sui generis* forms of protection for the same botanical genus or species, and the U.S. became signatory to the 1991 Act.[55] Notably, before becoming a member of the UPOV, the U.S. also had to make a number of revisions to the PPA, namely, the nomenclature requirement, provision of sample seed to the office, and changes to the experimental use provision.[56]

However, despite the effort to create a plant variety protection in conformity with the UPOV requirements, the protection provided by the PVPA appears to be limited. In 1985, the Senate Agriculture Committee asked the U.S. Department of Agriculture to evaluate the effect of the PVPA. The resulting report "The impacts of patent protection on the U.S. seed industry and public plant breeding"[57] was published in 1985. The report concluded that the PVPA had little impact on public sector research and significant, but selective, impact on private sector research. One of the major effects of the PVPA was the increased breeding activities of soybean and, to a lesser extent, wheat, while there has been little apparent effect on the breeding of other crops.[58]

Most scholars and practitioners agree that the PVPA had limited effect on the protection of plant varieties. Alston and Venner note that a number of provisions of the PVPA, such as "research exemption", "farmer exemption", meant that the

---

[52] U.S. Department of Agriculture. Plant Variety Protection <https://www.ams.usda.gov/services/plant-variety-protection> accessed 3 October 2022.

[53] Margaret Llewelyn and Mike Adcock 'European plant intellectual property' (n 12) 81.

[54] Margaret Llewelyn and Mike Adcock 'European plant intellectual property' (n 12) 80.

[55] USPTO. International Convention for the Protection of New Varieties of Plants<https://www.uspto.gov/ip-policy/patent-policy/international-convention-protection-new-varieties-plants> accessed 16 October 2022.

[56] Margaret Llewelyn and Mike Adcock 'European plant intellectual property' (n 12) 81.

[57] Leslie J. Butler and Bruce W. Marion, 'The impacts of patent protection on the U.S. seed industry and public plant breeding' (Research Division, College of Agricultural and Life Sciences, University of Wisconsin-Madison 1985).

[58] Leslie J. Butler and Bruce W. Marion, 'Has the Plant Variety Protection Act achieved its legislative intent?' (1984) 13 Journal of Agronomic Education 110.

protection afforded to the certificate holder was only partial and weaker than utility patent protection.[59]

Today, almost 40 years later, the effect of the PVPA remains to be quite modest. According to the PVPO factsheet published in March 2021, PVPO receives approximately 450 applications per year,[60] which is almost three times less the number of plant patent applications filed every year and almost six times less the number of titles for the CPVR granted to EU breeders annually.

For these reasons, utility patents remain a widely used instrument for plant variety protection in the U.S. This has been affirmed after the landmark decision of the Supreme Court in *Diamond v. Chakrabarty*,[61] ruling that microorganisms are patentable subject matter, and the decision by the Board of Patent Appeals and Interferences of the USPTO in *Ex parte Hibberd*,[62] holding that plants can be patented under the general patent statute.[63]

Before *Chakrabarty*, the provisions of 35 U.S.C. § 101 ("Whoever invents or discovers any new and useful process, machine, manufacture, or composition of matter, or any new and useful improvement thereof, may obtain a patent therefor, subject to the conditions and requirements of this title") were interpreted to exclude any living things. However, in *Chakrabarty*, it was argued whether the terms "manufacture" or "composition of matter" were meant to include living things, as, according to the USPTO, the PPA and the PVPA would not have been necessary if § 101 covered living things. However, the Supreme Court concluded that there was nothing in the language or history of these legal acts to suggest that they had been enacted because § 101 did not include living things. To the contrary, the Court held that "the relevant distinction was not between living and inanimate things, but between products of nature, whether living or not, and human-made inventions". Thus, Chakrabarty's microorganism, being the result of human ingenuity and research, is patentable subject matter.

After this landmark decision, the USPTO received patent applications not only for microorganisms, but also for plants. However, the patent commissioners were rejecting applications for plants, plant cells, and seeds, arguing that general patent law was inappropriate for protection of plants and even in conflict with the PPA and PVPA.[64]

Another landmark decision, *Ex parte Hibberd*, followed after a patent for "Tryptophan Overproducer Mutants of Cereal Crops" had been rejected in 1984. The USPTO's Board of Patent Appeals and Interferences held that there was nothing in

[59] Julian M. Alston and Raymond J. Venner, 'The effects of the US Plant Variety Protection Act on wheat genetic improvement' (2002) 31 Research Policy 527.

[60] U.S. Department of Agriculture. Plant Variety Protection <https://www.ams.usda.gov/sites/default/files/media/PlantVarietyProtectionFactsheet.pdf> accessed 17 October 2022.

[61] 447 U.S. 303 (1980).

[62] 227 U.S.P.Q. 443 (P.T.O. Bd. App. & Inter. 1985).

[63] Jennifer Van Brunt, 'Ex parte Hibberd: Another Landmark Decision' (1985) 3 Nature Biotechnology 1059.

[64] Ibid.

the legislative histories of the PPA and the PVPA to suggest that they preempted patent protection for plant subject matter.

Further, in 2001, the Supreme Court affirmed this position in *J. E. M. Ag Supply, Inc. v. Pioneer Hi-Bred International, Inc.*,[65] holding that "newly developed plant breeds fall within the terms of § 101, and that neither the PPA nor the PVPA limits the scope of § 101's coverage".

Thus, unlike in the EU, the utility patents are widely used for plant material protection in the U.S. Notably, the U.S. has granted the most patents over biological inventions. This is partially due to the fact that the U.S. patent system is based on the presumption of patentability and, unlike the European system, contains few limitations on the rights granted and has virtually no exclusions from protection.[66]

In sum, although the U.S. has three forms of legal rights available for the protection of plant varieties, which is more than in most of the UPOV member states, the protections granted under the PPA and the PVPA are limited, which is demonstrated by the number of applications for these rights, especially as compared to the number of applications for the CPVR in the EU. For these reasons, utility patents remain a widely used form of protection of new varieties of plants in the U.S.

4.3 Conclusions

Thus, *sui generis* protection for plant varieties is facilitated and encouraged by international agreements, such as the TRIPS Agreement and the UPOV Convention. The imperative to provide the population with food, as well as the objectives of safeguarding animal and plant life and the protection of the environment are some of the reasons why *sui generis* legal protection for plant varieties has been recognized at international level and implemented in various jurisdictions. Another reason is a common agreement, at least at the European level, that patent protection is not appropriate for plant varieties and that breeders require a special form of protection for their creations that would suit their needs.

Both the U.S. and the EU have implemented their own plant variety protection systems that have the primary objective of encouraging innovation in the breeding industry and development of new plant varieties, which is of utmost importance in the face of global food and nutrition crisis.[67] However, these systems and the available forms of protection are quite different.

---

[65] 534 U.S. 124 (2001).

[66] Margaret Llewelyn and Mike Adcock 'European plant intellectual property' (Oxford: Hart Publishing 2006) 89–90.

[67] Food and Agriculture Organization of the United Nations. The State of Food Security and Nutrition in the World 2022 <https://www.fao.org/publications/sofi/2022/en/> accessed 5 October 2022.

In the EU, the CPVR provides for a Community-wide breeder's right, existing along with the national plant variety protection systems. However, cumulative protection for the same plant material by both the CPVR and national systems is prohibited. Plant varieties and products derived from using essentially biological processes are also excluded from patent protection, which has been affirmed by the recent EPO practice.

In the U.S., special protection for plant breeders is provided under the PPA and the PVPA. However, both of these forms of protection are not widely used, since utility patents, that offer a stronger form of protection, have been available for the protection of plant material since the landmark Supreme Court and USPTO decisions.

Thus, the EU model of *sui generis* protection for plant varieties appears to be more effective and commonly used than that of the U.S., where utility patents remain a key instrument of plant material protection. This is, in part, due to the specifics of the U.S. patent law, namely, the presumption of patentability and nearly no exclusions from patent protection.

Chapter 5
Sui Generis Intellectual Property Protection for Works Generated by AI Systems

5.1 Intelligence v. Artificial Intelligence

There is no internationally agreed-upon definition of artificial intelligence. "Artificial intelligence" is an umbrella term used to refer to the ability of a digital computer or computer-controlled robot to perform tasks commonly associated with intelligent beings.[1] WIPO defines AI as a discipline of computer science which is aimed at developing machines and systems that can carry out tasks considered to require human intelligence.[2]

Thus, "intelligence" is the key factor that distinguishes AI from other software programs. It is therefore important to determine what is understood by "intelligence".

"Intelligence" can be defined as a mental quality that consists of the abilities to learn from experience, adapt to new situations, understand and handle abstract concepts, and use knowledge to manipulate one's environment.[3] Studying human intelligence currently lies in the domain of psychology. Interestingly, it is considered that it was French psychologist Binet who initiated the transfer of studying intelligence and "abnormal" from the domain of psychiatry to psychology. With equal access to knowledge being one of the cornerstones of the French Third Republic (1870–1940), a law making primary education compulsory for all children aged 6–13 years was enacted in 1882. As teachers were complaining of the presence of "slow" children in their classes, psychiatrist Bourneville suggested creating special schools for such children with "special needs", whereas Binet proposed to establish special classes for retarded children as an extension of the normal schools. In 1905, Binet, with his assistant Simon, presented a mental test establishing a progressive "metric"

---

[1] Britannica. Artificial intelligence <https://www.britannica.com/technology/artificial-intelligence> accessed 27 February 2023.

[2] WIPO. Frequently Asked Questions: AI and IP Policy. What is artificial intelligence? <https://www.wipo.int/about-ip/en/artificial_intelligence/faq.html> accessed 27 February 2023.

[3] Britannica. Human intelligence <https://www.britannica.com/science/human-intelligence-psychology/Psychometric-theories> accessed 02 March 2023.

I. Kazeeva, *Sui Generis Intellectual Property Protection*, Perspectives in Law, Business and Innovation, https://doi.org/10.1007/978-981-99-8897-6_5

scale of intelligence, known as the Binet-Simon scale. Binet eventually succeeded in making intelligence a psychological, rather than a psychiatric, object, as a new law establishing special classes for "slow" children attached to public schools was enacted in 1909, thus allying psychology with pedagogy.[4]

The Binet-Simon test was further introduced into American psychology with the translation into English by Goddard in 1910 and the Stanford Revision published by Terman in 1916.[5]

German psychologist Stern defined intelligence as "a general capacity of an individual consciously to adjust his thinking to new requirements: it is general mental adaptability to new problems and conditions of life".[6] Stern further explained that "the fact that the adjustment is made to the *new* distinguishes intelligence from *memory* whose fundamental teleological feature is the conservation and utilization of conscious contents already given".[7] Stern introduced the term "intelligence quotient" ("mental quotient"), which expresses the ratio of mental to chronological age, where mental age is a value indicating that the intelligence of the individual is equivalent to the average intelligence of individuals of the stated age, based on the individual's performance in the tests.[8]At the same time, Stern warned that, however good the intelligence tests were, they could not allow to gain full insight into human individuality, as volition and emotional factors are also highly relevant and individuals differ from one another not only quantitatively, but also qualitatively.[9]

The question whether machines have intelligence and can think has occupied people's minds for a long time. One of the first expressions of this dilemma in science fiction was the play "R.U.R." written by a Czech writer Čapek, introducing the word "robot", of Slavic origin, into other languages.

In 1950, English mathematician Turing published "Computing Machinery and Intelligence" that opened with the question "can machines think?" Instead of answering this question directly, which would require a person first to define the complex terms "think" and "machines", Turing suggested an imitation game where a human interrogator tries to guess which one of the other two participants is a machine.[10] This imitation game, the so-called Turing test, has been applied since

---

[4] Serge Nicolas, Bernard Andrieu, Jean-Claude Croizet, Rasyid B. Sanitioso, Jeremy Trevelyan Burman, 'Sick? Or slow? On the origins of intelligence as a psychological object' (2013) 41 Intelligence 699.

[5] Lewis M. Terman, *The Measurement of Intelligence. An Explanation of and a Complete Guide for the Use of the Stanford Revision and Extension of the Binet-Simon Intelligence Scale* (The Riverside Press 1916) in Ellwood P. Cubberley (ed) Riverside Textbooks in Education 2007 <https://www.gutenberg.org/files/20662/20662-h/20662-h.htm#CHAPTER_VIII> accessed 7 March 2023.

[6] William Stern, *The Psychological Methods of Testing Intelligence* (Guy M. Whipple tr, Warwick & York, Inc. 1914) 3.

[7] Ibid 3 (author's style preserved).

[8] Ibid 36–42.

[9] James T. Lamiell, *Beyond Individual and Group Differences: Human Individuality, Scientific Psychology, and William Stern's Critical Personalism* (Sage Publications 2003) 62.

[10] Alan M. Turing, 'Computing Machinery and Intelligence' (1950) Vol. Lix. No. 236 Mind. A Quarterly Review of Phycology and Philosophy 433.

then to test the state-of-the-art in artificial intelligence, including at Loebner Prize, an annual competition that continued until 2019.[11]

The term "artificial intelligence" was introduced in 1955 in a Proposal for the Dartmouth summer research project on artificial intelligence prepared by a research group including an American computer scientist McCarthy.[12] The basis for the study was "the conjecture that every aspect of learning or any other feature of intelligence can in principle be so precisely described that a machine can be made to simulate it."[13]

As technologies advanced and artificial intelligence gained more attention from both scholars and practitioners, it also gained thorough critique. American philosopher Dreyfus was one of the most prominent critics of artificial intelligence pointing out its limits and trying to demonstrate that the hopes and optimism related to the capabilities of artificial intelligence were largely misguided.[14] In "Mind Over Machine: The Power of Human Intuition and Expertise in the Era of the Computer" (1986),[15] Dreyfus, in co-authorship with his brother, a computer scientist, argues that human intuitive thinking could never be replicated by computers: intuitive thinkers notice changes around them "and alter their actions accordingly, without even conscious awareness of so doing. Because computers are not sensitive to the contexts in which they operate, they cannot detect similarities and differences between contexts, so they cannot acquire intuitions (i.e., learn to think intuitively)."[16]

With the fast development of artificial intelligence and machine learning that we have witnessed in the twenty-first century, artificial intelligence has been widely attributed outstanding capabilities, performing at the same level as, or superseding, humans in a wide range of fields.[17] Such advancement of artificial intelligence has led some scholars to assume that AI systems are approaching human qualities in a manner that entitles them to comparable recognition before the law, i.e., giving them legal personality.[18]

---

[11] Swansea University. 2019 Loebner Prize <https://www.swansea.ac.uk/computational-foundry/news/mitsuku-wins2019loebner-prize/> accessed 27 July 2023.

[12] John McCarthy, Marvin L. Minsky, Nathaniel Rochester, Claude E. Shannon, 'A Proposal for the Dartmouth summer research project on artificial intelligence' (1955) <http://jmc.stanford.edu/articles/dartmouth/dartmouth.pdf> accessed 27 July 2023.

[13] Ibid 2.

[14] See Hubert L. Dreyfus, *Alchemy and AI* (Rand Corporation 1965), Hubert L. Dreyfus, *What Computers Can't Do* (Harper & Row, Publishers 1972), Hubert L. Dreyfus, *What Computers Still Can't Do: A Critique of Artificial Reason* (The MIT Press 1992).

[15] Hubert L. Dreyfus, Stuart E. Dreyfus, *Mind Over Machine: The Power of Human Intuition and Expertise in the Era of the Computer* (The Free Press 1986).

[16] Sophie Haroutunian-Gordon, Review: Mind over Machine: A Plea for the Intuitive Conception of Mind (1988) 17 Educational Researcher 50.

[17] Stanford University. Gathering Strength, Gathering Storms: The One Hundred Year Study on Artificial Intelligence (AI100) 2021 Study Panel Report <https://ai100.stanford.edu/gathering-strength-gathering-storms-one-hundred-year-study-artificial-intelligence-ai100-2021-study> accessed 3 August 2023.

[18] Simon Chesterman, *We, the Robots? Regulating Artificial Intelligence and the Limits of the Law* (Cambridge University Press, 2021) 127.

However, these assumptions are subject to wide-ranging critique. Almost 50 years after having coined the term "artificial intelligence", McCarthy admitted that we are still far from creating human-level AI: "if we understood enough about how the human intellect works, we could simulate it. However, we don't have sufficient ability to observe ourselves or others to understand directly how our intellects work. Understanding the human brain well enough to imitate its function therefore requires theoretical and experimental success in psychology and neurophysiology."[19]

Smith points out that it is important to draw the line between "judgment" and "reckoning" to understand the difference between human thinking and AI. Smith applies the term "judgement" as an ideal to which human thinking must ultimately aspire, a capacity that we try to instill in our children, a form of dispassionate (fair, open-minded, without prejudice) deliberative thought, grounded in ethical commitment and responsible action, appropriate to the situation in which it is deployed.[20] Whereas "reckoning" is a calculative prowess, at which AI systems already excel, but that lack ethical commitment, deep contextual awareness, and ontological sensitivity of judgment.[21]

Lee opines that true intelligence requires life, including the possibility to replicate the genes responsible for its creation. Lee defines intelligence as the ability to solve complex problems or make decisions with outcomes benefiting the actor. It allows humans and many animals to identify complex objects and produce agile behaviours in many different ways and in many different situations. Lee points out that the development of AI has been facilitated by the advances in the neuroscience research in the recent years. Creating artificial general intelligence would require an even better understanding of the human brain. Thus, Lee considers, the creation of superintelligence is unlikely to happen in the near future and, until then, machines will always only be surrogates of human intelligence.[22]

The tests that are applied to assess the capabilities of AI systems reveal their weaknesses and demonstrate that even the best AI systems are still not able to simulate human thinking. The testing of the Generative Pre-trained Transformer 4 (GPT-4),[23] released by a California-based AI research company OpenAI in March 2023, has revealed that this OpenAI's most advanced system still falls short of the thinking capabilities of an average human. For instance, after testing humans and state-of-the-art machine solvers, researchers have reported that "humans substantially outperform the machine solvers ... showing abilities to abstract and generalize concepts that

---

19 John McCarthy, 'From Here to Human-Level AI' (2007) 171 Artificial Intelligence 1174.

20 Brian C. Smith, *The Promise of Artificial Intelligence. Reckoning and Judgment* (The MIT Press 2019) xv.

21 Ibid xvii.

22 Johns Hopkins Medicine. Q&A – What Is Intelligence? (discussion with Daeyeol Lee, 5 October 2020) <https://www.hopkinsmedicine.org/news/articles/qa--what-is-intelligence> accessed 1 March 2023.

23 OpenAI. GPT-4 is OpenAI's most advanced system, producing safer and more useful responses <https://openai.com/gpt-4> accessed 4 August 2023.

are not yet captured by AI systems".[24] Another research, where the mathematical capabilities of ChatGPT were tested, demonstrated that its "overall mathematical performance is well below the level of a graduate student".[25]

It is therefore important, when speaking of any form of legal regulation for AI, not to be confused by the name "artificial intelligence", as it is still very far from human thinking capabilities. After all, one of the reasons for introducing such a name was simply to escape association with "cybernetics."[26] However, regardless of the name, the question whether and how the works generated by AI should be protected by intellectual property law remains valid.

5.2 Artificial Intelligence and Intellectual Property Law

In order to answer the question of intellectual property protection for AI-generated works, it is worth looking at such works through the lens of the theories of intellectual property law.

As described in Sect. 1.1 of this volume, there are two groups of rationales behind the concept of intellectual property: natural rights theories and the incentive (utilitarian) theories.

For natural rights theories, which include labor theory and personality theory, the key element is the concept of a person's will. Intellectual property is seen as embodiment of a person's will and labor into other objects. However, the foregoing analysis of intelligence as a psychological notion and of the current state of AI has demonstrated that AI is still very far from human intelligence, hence both labor and personality theories are inapplicable for granting intellectual property rights to AI systems. As to the creators and inventors, it is arguable to what extent the works generated by AI systems are the extension and embodiment of the creators' and inventors' will and labor. As Hilty, Hoffmann, and Scheuerer point out, with the fast-moving development of AI, the human involvement is expected to constantly decrease, thus the relevance of deontological justification theories in the AI field,

---

[24] Arseny Moskvichev, Victor Vikram Odouard, Melanie Mitchell, "The ConceptARC Benchmark: Evaluating Understanding and Generalization in the ARC Domain" arXiv preprint, submitted on 11 May 2023 <https://arxiv.org/abs/2305.07141> accessed 4 August 2023. See also Celeste Biever, 'ChatGPT broke the Turing test—the race is on for new ways to assess AI. Large language models mimic human chatter, but scientists disagree on their ability to reason' Nature, 25 July 2023 <https://www.nature.com/articles/d41586-023-02361-7> accessed 3 August 2023.

[25] Simon Frieder, Luca Pinchetti1, Alexis Chevalier, Ryan-Rhys Griffiths, Tommaso Salvatori, Thomas Lukasiewicz, Philipp Christian Petersen, Julius Berner, "Mathematical Capabilities of ChatGPT" arXiv preprint, submitted on 31 January 2023 < https://arxiv.org/abs/2301.13867> accessed 4 August 2023.

[26] John McCarthy, *Defending AI Research: A Collection of Essays and Reviews* (CSLI Publications 1996).

for both AI tools and AI outputs, will constantly diminish. Therefore, the potential protection regimes will be looking not at creators or inventors, but at investors.[27]

Incentive (utilitarian) theories can be divided into general incentive theory and investment protection theory. The former is entrenched in deontological and psychological considerations, whereas the latter serves to protect investors from imitators who can save on product development costs and offer identical products cheaper, thus undermining the return of the investments made into the initial product. Hilty, Hoffmann, and Scheuerer write that the general incentive theory loses its relevance in the context of AI, since the AI tool is not conscious of, or responsive to, economic incentives. As regards human actors (programmer, user of AI tool, distributor of AI outputs), firstly, their incentives are already taken into account (e.g., by IP protection for specific elements of AI tools or by sales and licensing revenues), and, secondly, there is obviously no lack of motivation to be active in these areas.

As to the investment protection theory, Hilty, Hoffmann, and Scheuerer analyze that, in the case of AI tools, intellectual property protection does not seem justifiable, due to low likelihood of misappropriation and strong technical protection measures. However, for AI outputs, intellectual property protection based on protection of investments may be justifiable, because technical protection measures for AI outputs may not exist and misappropriation might be possible.[28]

Depending on AI system, there may be different investments in AI, such as high-quality data, infrastructure, computing power, know-how.[29] Among these components, data are one of the most novel forms of investment. Data are used at all the stages of AI development, including training, testing, evaluation, and deployment, being one of the main drivers behind the development of AI technologies. Availability (whether data exist) and accessibility (whether data are accessible), as well as the quality of data, play an important role in the development of AI systems.[30]

The wide use of data for AI development poses a number of legal challenges, including in the fields of privacy and intellectual property rights.

The right to privacy is recognized as a human right at international level. Both the Universal Declaration of Human Rights (Article 12)[31] and International Covenant on

---

[27] Reto M. Hilty, Jörg Hoffmann, Stefan Scheuerer, 'Intellectual Property Justification for Artificial Intelligence' in Jyh-An Lee, Reto Hilty, Kung-Chung Liu (eds) *Artificial Intelligence and Intellectual Property* (Oxford University Press 2021).

[28] Ibid 61–72.

[29] Ibid 64.

[30] The Role of Data in AI. Report for the Data Governance Working Group of the Global Partnership of AI. Digital Curation Centre. Trilateral Research. School of Informatics, the University of Edinburgh. November 2020 <https://gpai.ai/projects/data-governance/role-of-data-in-ai.pdf> accessed 8 August 2023.

[31] United Nations Human Rights Office of the High Commissioner. Universal Declaration of Human Rights <https://www.ohchr.org/en/human-rights/universal-declaration/translations/english> accessed 11 August 2023.

Civil and Political Rights (Article 17)[32] state that no one shall be subjected to arbitrary interference with his privacy, family, home, or correspondence, nor to attacks upon his honor and reputation. Although the right to privacy is not absolute, everyone has the right to the protection of the law against such interference or attacks. Data protection standards differ depending on jurisdiction, which, in turn, influences the accessibility of data for AI development. A number of cases filed in the U.S. against largest AI developers reveal the challenges posed by AI training to privacy. In *P.M. v. OpenAI LP*,[33] plaintiffs allege that OpenAI used personally identifiable information of millions of internet users, including children of all ages, without their informed consent or knowledge, to train OpenAI's products. In *L. v. Alphabet Inc.*,[34] plaintiffs assert that their private information that they shared with Google products and services was used to train AI products like "Bard", a chatbot released by Google to compete with OpenAI's ChatGPT.

Availability of data for AI is also dependent on intellectual property rights in such data. Data can be protected by copyright and (or) *sui generis* database rights, the latter rights existing, besides the EU, in India, South Africa, and South Korea.[35] Intellectual property rights in data used for AI development pose the question whether AI-generated works should be considered as derivative works from such protected data. This is being claimed in *Andersen et al. v. Stability AI et al.*,[36] a case brought against AI platforms by three artists arguing that their original works had been used to create AI-generated images. Another case is *Kadrey v. Meta Platforms, Inc.*,[37] where Meta Platforms Inc. is sued by a group of authors claiming that their copyrighted books were used for training of Meta's LLaMA, a set of large language models released in February 2023. A number of similar cases have been filed against OpenAI for having allegedly used copyrighted works in ChatGPT training.[38]

Although AI developers could potentially rely on the fair use doctrine, arguing that AI products are transformative uses of expressive data, courts might disagree on the ground that the work's original purpose is not altered in the process of compiling the training data set. Quang suggests that data mining safe harbor should be introduced in the U.S. copyright law in order to dissolve this uncertainty. According to Quang, use of data for AI development is not an act of infringement, because the protected data are not redistributed or recommunicated to the public, and downloading such data for

[32] United Nations Human Rights Office of the High Commissioner. International Covenant on Civil and Political Rights <https://www.ohchr.org/en/instruments-mechanisms/instruments/international-covenant-civil-and-political-rights> accessed 11 August 2023.

[33] *P.M. v. OpenAI LP*, 3:23-cv-03199, (N.D. Cal.).

[34] *L. v. Alphabet Inc.*, 3:23-cv-03440, (N.D. Cal.).

[35] The Role of Data in AI. Report for the Data Governance Working Group of the Global Partnership of AI (n 30).

[36] *Andersen v. Stability AI Ltd.*, 3:23-cv-00201, (N.D. Cal.).

[37] *Kadrey v. Meta Platforms, Inc.*, 3:23-cv-03417, (N.D. Cal.).

[38] See, e.g., cases *Tremblay v. OpenAI, Inc.*, 3:23-cv-03223, (N.D. Cal.), *Silverman v. OpenAI, Inc.*, 3:23-cv-03416, (N.D. Cal.).

AI training purposes is essentially making copies for technical or non-communicative uses, which is different from the work's expressive purpose.[39]

In the EU, such safe harbor for data mining was introduced with the Digital Single Market Directive, namely the exception for the purposes of scientific research (Article 3) and the exception or limitation for commercial use (Article 4). Notably, in the latter case, rightholders can reverse (opt out from) such use of their works. Moreover, the proposed AI Act requires providers of generative AI models to "document and make publicly available a sufficiently detailed summary of the use of training data protected under copyright law" (Article 28b(4)(c)).[40] Japan also has exceptions for text and data mining, being the first country in the world to have introduced such changes into its copyright laws.[41]

Despite the legal challenges, the world's largest technology companies make significant investments into AI development.[42] Thus, the works generated by AI models, in case investments have been made, may be eligible for intellectual property protection, since no other protection measures may be available.[43]

5.3 Intellectual Property Protection for AI-Generated Works

As it has been demonstrated in the foregoing section, works generated by AI models may be eligible for intellectual property protection based on the rationale of protecting the investments made into the development of such AI models. This section aims to analyze which form of intellectual property rights is more suitable for the protection of AI-generated works and whether a special, *sui generis*, form of protection might be the best solution to protect AI outputs.

Within the traditional framework of intellectual property rights, AI-generated works might most probably be eligible for protection by copyright or patents.

In copyright law, the two key concepts forming the requirements for copyright protection are "authorship" and "originality". The Berne Convention repeatedly

---

[39] Jenny Quang, 'Does Training AI Violate Copyright Law?' (2021) 36 Berkeley Technology Law Journal 1407.

[40] European Parliament. P9_TA(2023)0236. Artificial Intelligence Act. Amendments adopted by the European Parliament on 14 June 2023 on the proposal for a regulation of the European Parliament and of the Council on laying down harmonized rules on artificial intelligence (Artificial Intelligence Act) and amending certain Union legislative acts (COM(2021)0206—C9-0146/2021—2021/0106(COD)) <https://www.europarl.europa.eu/doceo/document/TA-9-2023-0236_EN.pdf> accessed 14 August 2023.

[41] Jenny Quang, 'Does Training AI Violate Copyright Law?' (n 39) 1431.

[42] Financial Times. Google invests $300 mn in artificial intelligence start-up Anthropic (3 February 2023) <https://www.ft.com/content/583ead66-467c-4bd5-84d0-ed5df7b5bf9c> accessed 16 August 2023.

[43] See Reto M. Hilty, Jörg Hoffmann, Stefan Scheuerer, 'Intellectual Property Justification for Artificial Intelligence'(n 27).

mentions "original" works, which are generally assumed to imply a requirement of human intellectual effort or creativity. Besides, the text and historical context of the Convention strongly suggest that "author" and "authorship" refer to the natural person who created the work.[44] Although the concept of work is not harmonized under EU copyright law, it makes specific references to the Berne Convention in both secondary[45] and CJEU case law.[46] Generally speaking, both the Berne Convention and EU copyright law are grounded in the tradition of author's rights (*droit d'auteur*): the protected works should emanate from a human creator and be the result of human intellectual effort.[47]

Similar to the EU, the U.S. copyright law protects original works of authorship, meaning that such works must be created by a human being. On this ground, the U.S. Copyright Office will not register works produced by nature, animals, or plants, as well as by machines or mere mechanical process that operates randomly or automatically without any creative input or intervention from a human author.[48] This requirement was confirmed in the statement of policy issued by the U.S. Copyright Office in March 2023, clarifying its practices for examining and registering works that contain material generated by the use of AI technology.[49] In the guidance for copyright applicants, the Copyright Office advises that "individuals who use AI technology in creating a work may claim copyright protection for their own contributions to that work".[50]

Under patent law, the application for registration should designate an inventor (Article 81 of the EPC, 35 U.S.C. §115(a)). The notorious case that challenged the inventorship requirement in both the EU and U.S. is the one involving an AI system DABUS, where applicants attempted to register an invention created autonomously by DABUS. In its decision, the Legal Board of Appeal of the EPO confirmed the decisions of the Receiving Section to refuse the applications for registration on the ground that only a human being could be an inventor within the meaning of the

---

[44] European Commission. Trends and Developments in Artificial Intelligence. Challenges to the Intellectual Property Rights Framework. Publications Office of the European Union, 2020 <https://op.europa.eu/en/publication-detail/-/publication/394345a1-2ecf-11eb-b27b-01aa75ed71a1/language-en> accessed 17 August 2023.

[45] E.g., Article 1 of Directive 2006/116/EC of the European Parliament and of the Council of 12 December 2006 on the term of protection of copyright and certain related rights [2006] OJ L 372 refers to "a literary or artistic work within the meaning of Article 2 of the Berne Convention".

[46] See, e.g., Case C-5/08 *Infopaq International A/S v Danske Dagblades Forening* [2009] ECR I-06569 paras 11 and 34.

[47] European Commission. Trends and Developments in Artificial Intelligence. Challenges to the Intellectual Property Rights Framework (n 44).

[48] U.S. Copyright Office, Compendium of U.S. Copyright Office Practices § 101 (3d ed. 2021) Sect. 313.2.

[49] Federal Register. Copyright Registration Guidance: Works Containing Material Generated by Artificial Intelligence. 16 March 2023 <https://www.federalregister.gov/documents/2023/03/16/2023-05321/copyright-registration-guidance-works-containing-material-generated-by-artificial-intelligence> accessed 17 August 2023.

[50] Ibid.

EPC.[51] The USPTO also denied registration stating that the current statutes, case law, and USPTO regulations and rules limit inventorship to natural persons.[52] The only jurisdiction where DABUS as inventor was granted a patent is South Africa. However, the examination of patent applications in South Africa is limited, as it focuses mainly on documentation, financial, and administrative issues, ignoring the questions whether the invention is designated as excluded subject matter and whether the inventor and applicant are qualified persons. Hence, it is believed that it is unlikely that the DABUS patent will withstand a validity test if judicially scrutinized, since it offends the provisions of the South African Patent Act and runs contrary to the human-centered stance of the South African patent regime.[53]

Besides the formal requirements, there may be challenges in applying patentability requirements, such as novelty, susceptibility of industrial application, and inventive step, to AI outputs. Furthermore, the requirements regarding the disclosure of the invention sufficiently clear for it to be carried out by a person skilled in the art might be difficult to satisfy (Article 83 EPC and a similar duty of disclosure in the U.S. under 37 CFR §1.56).[54] Interestingly, according to the assessment of the EPO, the invention that DABUS was claimed to have invented (food or beverage container) does not involve an inventive step and the description of the invention lacks sufficiency.[55]

A legal regime that is similar to copyright, but applying less strict standards, is related rights, as they do not require originality or authorship. In its report on the challenges to the intellectual property rights framework posed by artificial intelligence, the European Commission concludes that related rights may be suitable for the protection of AI outputs in the sectors of audio recording, broadcasting, audiovisual recording, and news.[56] The feature that these rights have in common is that their rationale lies not in the creativeness, but rather in the financial and organizational investments.

The phonographic right is triggered by the fact of fixation of sounds and vests in the producer of the phonogram, meaning "the person, or the legal entity, who or which takes the initiative and has the responsibility for the first fixation of the sounds

---

[51] J 8/20 (Designation of inventor/DABUS) 21–12-2021 and J 9/20 (Designation of inventor/DABUS II) 21–12-2021.

[52] In re Application No. 16/524,350, Decision on Petition, 22 April 2020 <https://www.uspto.gov/sites/default/files/documents/16524350_22apr2020.pdf> accessed 17 August 2023.

[53] Desmond O. Oriakhogba, 'Dabus Gains Territory in South Africa and Australia: Revisiting the AI-Inventorship Question' (2021) 9 South African Intellectual Property Law Journal 87.

[54] For a detailed discussion on these challenges see European Commission. Trends and Developments in Artificial Intelligence. Challenges to the Intellectual Property Rights Framework (n 44) 106–114.

[55] See Annex to the Communication pursuant to Article 94(3) EPC dated 14 March 2023, Section 25. Application No. 21216024.6 < https://register.epo.org/application?documentId=LF1C0ZT2L0RQODK&number=EP21216024&lng=en&npl=false > accessed 18 August 2023.

[56] European Commission. Trends and Developments in Artificial Intelligence. Challenges to the Intellectual Property Rights Framework (n 44) 88–92.

of a performance or other sounds, or the representations of sounds".[57] Thus, with respect to AI, the phonographic right would be allocated to the user as the person taking the initiative to fixate the sounds.

Broadcasting is the transmission by wireless means for public reception of sounds or of images and sounds.[58] The prerequisite for the right is the act of broadcasting of audio or audiovisual content. Accordingly, with respect to AI, the right will emerge if the content is broadcast by an AI system.

The film producer's right grants legal protection to producers of a first fixation of films.[59] Thus, it would allow protection of video content produced by AI systems.

Under the press publisher's right, introduced by the Digital Single Market Directive, AI outputs could be protected as long as they fit into the definition of press publication: "a collection composed mainly of literary works of a journalistic nature, but which can also include other works or other subject matter, and which: (a) constitutes an individual item within a periodical or regularly updated publication under a single title, such as a newspaper or a general or special interest magazine; (b) has the purpose of providing the general public with information related to news or other topics; and (c) is published in any media under the initiative, editorial responsibility and control of a service provider".[60]

Related rights in AI outputs, per the European Commission, should be allocated to the user, not the developer, of the AI system. However, such allocation of the right to the user does not appear to be in line with the initial rationale of these related rights, which is based in the idea of recovering the financial and organizational investments made by producers and broadcasting organizations. With the advancement of technologies, the costs of producing phonograms and of broadcasting have significantly decreased, which has raised the question whether these rights are still justified, especially since, unlike copyright or *sui generis* database right, related rights do not provide for a threshold requirement.[61] Accordingly, it is doubtful whether an AI user would make any substantive investment to achieve a certain AI output that would require protection with a related right. Furthermore, as noted above, there is obviously no lack of motivation for AI users to use AI systems producing AI outputs,

---

[57] Article 2(d) of the WIPO Performances and Phonograms Treaty (1996) <https://www.wipo.int/treaties/en/ip/wppt/> accessed 21 August 2023. The Rome Convention provides a similar definition: "the person who, or the legal entity which, first fixes the sounds of a performance or other sounds" (Article 3(c)).

[58] Article 3(f) of the Rome Convention.

[59] Directive 2006/115/EC of the European Parliament and of the Council of 12 December 2006 on rental right and lending right and on certain rights related to copyright in the field of intellectual property [2006] OJ L376/28; Articles 2(d) and 3(2)(c) of the Directive 2001/29/EC of the European Parliament and of the Council of 22 May 2001 on the harmonisation of certain aspects of copyright and related rights in the information society [2001] OJ L167.

[60] Article 2(4) of the Digital Single Market Directive.

[61] P. Bernt Hugenholtz, 'Neighbouring Rights are Obsolete' 2019 <https://link.springer.com/content/pdf/10.1007/s40319-019-00864-3.pdf> accessed 27 November 2021.

therefore it is questionable whether AI users need such incentives in the form of a special intellectual property right to continue using AI systems.[62]

Another legal regime not imposing the authorship requirement is the EU database right. AI outputs could be protected by the *sui generis* database right, provided that such outputs qualify as database, i.e., a collection of independent works, data, or other materials arranged in a systematic or methodical way and individually accessible by electronic or other means.[63] According to the European Commission, the substantial investment requirement could be satisfied with the investments made into developing and implementing the AI system. However, it is uncertain whether databases consisting of machine-generated data can qualify for the *sui generis* right due to the creation/obtaining of data distinction established by the CJEU case law (see Sect. 2.1 of this volume).[64]

Due to the obstacles to protecting AI outputs by copyright, patent, or related rights, some scholars have proposed creating a special *sui generis* regime for the protection of AI-generated works. De Cock Buning writes that introduction of a *sui generis* right for the protection of AI outputs is a very likely option, as it would leave room for the attribution of rights that is most suitable: whether the beneficiary is the legal entity that made the investment into the AI system or the legal entity to be established in order to represent the AI system's acts in law.[65] Lorenzoni proposes a *sui generis* system for AI outputs that would protect works of art and inventions under the same regime. Per Lorenzoni, works of art, autonomously created by an AI system, for which investments have been made, and that are original, meaning they are not copies of existing works, would be protected by the *sui generis* system and, similar to copyright, not require registration. AI-generated inventions would be protected if they satisfy the requirements of novelty, industrial application, and "innovative step" (instead of an inventive step for patents), meaning the invention should be different from the prior art and such difference should make a substantial contribution to the working of the invention. For both works of art and inventions, Lorenzoni proposes a term of protection in between that offered to software and databases, e.g., 10 years. Similar to the *sui generis* database right, the *sui generis* right in AI outputs would be allocated to the person taking the initiative and the risk of investing into the AI system.[66] Despite the detailed description of the proposed *sui generis* system, it is not clear how the two regimes, which are essentially a copyright-like protection and a regime similar to utility patents, are to be combined into a single *sui generis* regime.

As noted above, protection of AI-generated works is most likely to be justifiable in case it is aimed at protecting the investments made into the AI systems. Such

---

[62] Reto M. Hilty, Jörg Hoffmann, Stefan Scheuerer, 'Intellectual Property Justification for Artificial Intelligence' (n 27).

[63] Article 1(2) of the Database Directive.

[64] European Commission. Trends and Developments in Artificial Intelligence. Challenges to the Intellectual Property Rights Framework (n 44) 92–94.

[65] Madeleine de Cock Buning, 'Autonomous Intelligent Systems as Creative Agents under the EU framework for Intellectual Property' (2016) 7 European Journal of Risk Regulation 310.

[66] Isabella Lorenzoni, 'Artificial Intelligence Creates, Invents … and Challenges Intellectual Property Law' (2020) 3 Stockholm Intellectual Property Law Review 26.

rationale for protecting AI outputs is similar to the one for protection of unoriginal databases in the EU, aimed at protecting the investments made into collecting and organizing the data into a database. Additionally, similar to the database right and in order to avoid the questions of overprotection as with related rights (in cases of recording or broadcasting requiring little to no investments), the *sui generis* right for AI outputs should provide for a minimum threshold for investments made into AI systems. However, as Ginsburg and Budiardjo argue, there is firstly a need for empirical evidence before upholding or declining the idea for a special intellectual property regime covering such authorless works as AI outputs.[67]

5.4 Conclusions

Thus, although the latest AI systems demonstrate capabilities that are seemingly equal to, or even supersede, those of humans, we are still very far from creating an AI system that would possess intelligence akin to human intelligence. The latter is characterized by ethical commitment and responsible action, appropriate for each unique situation. Creating a general artificial intelligence requires a thorough understanding of the human brain. Although the advances made in neuroscience have facilitated the developments that we now see in AI technologies, it is still unlikely that superintelligence, able to simulate human brain and behavior, will be created in the near future.

Referring to the theories justifying intellectual property rights allows to find the appropriate rationale for granting intellectual property protection to AI-generated works. AI systems themselves cannot (at least, at the moment) be granted intellectual property rights under either natural rights or incentive theories: in the case of natural rights theories, AI outputs cannot be considered embodiment of AI's will and labor and, in the case of incentive theories, AI systems are not conscious of, or responsive to, economic incentives. As to human actors, it is more likely that the potential protection regime should be addressed not at inventors or users, since their involvement in AI outputs is expected to continue diminishing (in case of natural rights theories), their interests are already protected by other means and they do not lack incentives to remain active in the field (in case of incentive theories). Thus, protection of AI-generated works would be most justifiable if based on the protection of investments made into AI systems.

Trying to find the appropriate form of intellectual property protection for AI outputs is a challenging task. Under copyright law, AI outputs do not meet the prerequisites of authorship and originality. Under patent law, the requirements of inventorship, as well as those of novelty, susceptibility of industrial application, inventive step, and sufficient disclosure, are either impossible or difficult to satisfy. Related rights, such as phonographic or broadcasting rights, are usually allocated to

[67] Jane C. Ginsburg, Luke Ali Budiardjo, 'Authors and Machines' (2019) 34 Berkeley Technology Law Journal 343.

the persons taking the initiative to fixate the sounds or to broadcast content. Accordingly, related rights in AI outputs would be granted to the user, which would not be in line with the rationale of protecting investments made into AI systems and of incentivizing innovation. The EU *sui generis* database right might apply only in case AI outputs are recognized as a database in the sense of the Database Directive. Thus, introducing a *sui generis* regime for the protection of AI outputs might be a viable solution, since no other means of protection are available for such works. The creation of such a regime is, however, subject to the following conditions: (1) the *sui generis* regime should be aimed at protection of investments made into AI systems, (2) there should be a minimum threshold for the investments made in order for AI outputs to qualify for such protection, and (3) the introduction of a new regime should be upheld by economic evidence demonstrating that such *sui generis* rights are crucial for incentivizing investments in AI technologies.

Conclusion

This book has demonstrated that the *sui generis* intellectual property regimes *de facto* serve as gap fillers for the protection of subject matter that cannot be adequately protected with the standard instruments of intellectual property protection.

The analysis of *sui generis* intellectual property protection for databases, designs, and plant varieties in the EU and U.S. allows to make the following conclusions:

1. Introduction of *sui generis* rights does not always trigger innovation and public or private investment into the protected subject matter. It is generally considered that the introduction of new intellectual property rights helps enhance innovation. However, this book has demonstrated that this has not always been the case. In particular, the database *sui generis* right in the EU has not had any proven economic impact on the production of databases. The introduction of a design right specifically for vessel hulls under the VHDPA and granting a plant variety right under the PVPA in the U.S. have not had significant impact on the amount of investments or innovation in these areas.
2. Among the three case studies, plant varieties have been the subject matter, for which *sui generis* form of intellectual property protection has been most recognized. The imperative to provide the population with food, the objectives of safeguarding animal and plant life, as well as the common acknowledgement (at least in Europe) that patents are not an adequate instrument for the protection of plant material are the main reasons why plant varieties have been a more "successful" subject matter, as compared to databases and designs, in gaining *sui generis* legal protection in different jurisdictions, as well as at international level.
3. The number of applications for the *sui generis* regimes depends not only on its merits, but also on the availability of other forms of protection. One of the evaluation criteria for the *sui generis* intellectual property regimes is the number of applications filed for the *sui generis* protection versus the applications filed for standard intellectual property regimes' protection. However, a large number of applications for *sui generis* protection might not just demonstrate the success

I. Kazeeva, *Sui Generis Intellectual Property Protection*, Perspectives in Law, Business and Innovation, https://doi.org/10.1007/978-981-99-8897-6

of this legal regime, but rather be due to the fact that no other forms of protection are available for the applicants. For instance, in the U.S., the availability of utility patents, which provide a stronger form of protection for plant varieties than the PPA or PVPA, affects the number of applications for the specific plant variety right.[1] At the same time, the availability of different forms of protection for databases in the U.S. is one of the reasons why a *sui generis* right for database owners has not been, and is not likely to be, introduced in this country. Whereas, in the EU, the *sui generis* database right, the Community design rights, and the CPVR are the only available forms of Community-wide protection for databases, designs, and plant varieties, respectively, which also contributes to the demand for these legal regimes.

4. *Sui generis* rights do not prove to be effective when granted to a very narrowly defined subject matter. In particular, there appears to be no demand for the vessel hull design right in the U.S., with no registration applications in the last decade. In contrast, the EU *sui generis* design rights provide protection for much broader defined categories of subject matter, allowing for creations in various industries to be granted *sui generis* protection.
5. *Sui generis* rights prove to be particularly effective when applied to introduce a supra-national (Community-wide) form of protection with a view to provide a harmonized regulation for a particular subject matter. One of the main objectives of the *sui generis* database right, the Community design rights, and the CPVR was to introduce a Community-wide right that would provide a harmonized protection across the Member States and facilitate a single market in the EU. According to the reports evaluating each of these three rights, this objective has been successfully fulfilled.
6. *Sui generis* regime for AI-generated works may be justifiable in case such regime is aimed at the protection of investments made into AI systems and the rights are allocated to the investors. Besides, the *sui generis* regime should provide for a minimum threshold for the investments made in order for AI outputs to qualify for such protection. However, the introduction of the new regime should be upheld by economic evidence demonstrating that such *sui generis* rights are crucial for incentivizing investments in AI technologies.

The conclusions listed above indicate that the success of *sui generis* intellectual property rights to a great extent depends on the subject matter that is granted protection, the territorial scope of the protection, historical background, as well as the availability of other forms of intellectual property protection for the chosen subject matter.

---

[1] Such is also the most probable explanation of the high number of design law applications in Japan, where designers have no other option, given that no recourse is provided by either copyright or unfair competition laws. See Estelle Derclaye, 'A Model Copyright/Design Interface: Not an Impossible and Undesirable Task?' in Estelle Derclaye (ed), *The Copyright/Design Interface: Past, Present and Future* (Cambridge University Press 2018) 421, 432.

The answer to the question whether to grant *sui generis* form of intellectual property protection to other subject matter or not will also depend on other available incentives. As correctly noted, there can be alternative mechanisms for rewarding creativity and innovation, which could be suitable especially for the subject matter not fully covered by the standard intellectual property legal regimes (such as prizes, governmental grants, other public sponsorship).[2]

At the same time, *sui generis* rights might be an appropriate regime for protection of the newest and most modern subject matter, which had not been foreseen at the stage of creation of the standard intellectual property regimes, such as AI outputs and other creations associated with the advancement of technologies in the digital age. The suitability and application of *sui generis* intellectual property rights for such newly emerging subject matter is still to be examined.

[2] Nancy Gallini and Suzanne Scotchmer, 'Intellectual Property: When Is It the Best Incentive System?' (2002) Innovation Policy and the Economy 2, 51.

References

Bibliography

AIPPI (2022) Study Guidelines 2016—study question (Designs) requirements for protection of designs. http://www.aippi.ch/wp-content/uploads/2018/01/AIPPI-Milan-Designs-Guidelines-FINAL-1.pdf. Accessed 18 Aug 2022

Alston JM, Venner RJ (2002) The effects of the US Plant Variety Protection Act on wheat genetic improvement. Res Policy 31:527

Beltrametti S (2010) Evaluation of the Design Piracy Prohibition Act: is the cure worse than the disease? An analogy with counterfeiting and a comparison with the protection available in the European Community. Northwest J Technol Intellect Property 8:147

Biever C (2023) ChatGPT broke the Turing test—the race is on for new ways to assess AI. Large language models mimic human chatter, but scientists disagree on their ability to reason. Nature, 25 July 2023. https://www.nature.com/articles/d41586-023-02361-7. Accessed 3 Aug 2023

Bizer K, Lankau M, Spindler G, Zimbehl P (2017) Sui generis rights for the protection of traditional cultural expressions: policy implications. In: Bizer K, Lankau M, Spindler G (eds) Sui generis Rechte zum Schutz traditioneller kultureller Ausdrucksweisen. Göttingen University Press, Göttingen, p 131

Brean DH (2008) Enough is enough: time to eliminate design patents and rely on more appropriate copyright and trademark protection for product designs. Texas Intellect Proper Law J 16:325

Britannica. Artificial intelligence. https://www.britannica.com/technology/artificial-intelligence. Accessed 27 Feb 2023

Britannica. Human intelligence. https://www.britannica.com/science/human-intelligence-psychology/Psychometric-theories. Accessed 2 Mar 2023

Burk DL (2000) The trouble with trespass. J Small Emerg Bus Law 4:27

Butler LJ, Marion BW (1984) Has the plant variety protection act achieved its legislative intent? J Agron Educ 13:110

Butler LJ, Marion BW (1985) The impacts of patent protection on the U.S. seed industry and public plant breeding. Research Division, College of Agricultural and Life Sciences, University of Wisconsin-Madison

Carter-Silk A, Lewiston M (2012) The development of design law—past and future: from history to policy. The Intellectual Property Office, p 15. https://assets.publishing.service.gov.uk/government/uploads/system/uploads/attachment_data/file/310380/ipresearch-designlaw-201207.pdf. Accessed 30 Nov 2021

I. Kazeeva, *Sui Generis Intellectual Property Protection*, Perspectives in Law, Business and Innovation, https://doi.org/10.1007/978-981-99-8897-6

Chesterman S (2021) We, the Robots? Regulating artificial intelligence and the limits of the law. Cambridge University Press, Cambridge, p 127
Clark C (2000) Net law: a cyberspace agenda for publishers. J World Intellect Proper 3:97. https://ur.booksc.eu/book/10123267/8c60f9. Accessed 24 Jan 2022
Cornish WR (1993) The international relations of intellectual property. Cambr Law J 52(1):46
Correa CM (2016) Sui generis protection for farmers' varieties. In: Halewood M (ed) Farmers' crop varieties and farmers' rights. Challenges in taxonomy and law. Routledge, London
David S (2016) European Union design law: a practitioners' guide. Oxford University Press, Oxford
Davison M (2017) Database protection: lessons from Europe, Congress, and WIPO. Case West Reserve Law Rev 57:829–852
de Cock Buning M (2016) Autonomous intelligent systems as creative agents under the EU framework for Intellectual Property. Eur J Risk Regul 7:310
Derclaye E (ed) (2018) The copyright/design interface: past, present and future. Cambridge University Press, Cambridge
Derclaye E (2007) Can and should misappropriation also protect databases? A comparative approach. In: Torremans P (ed) Copyright law: a handbook of contemporary research. Edward Elgar, Cheltenham
Drahos P (2021) A philosophy of intellectual property (ANU eText). https://press-files.anu.edu.au/downloads/press/n1902/html/ch03.xhtml#footnote-219. Accessed 28 Dec 2021
Dreyfus HL (1965) Alchemy and AI. Rand Corporation
Dreyfus HL, Dreyfus SE (1986) Mind over machine: the power of human intuition and expertise in the era of the computer. The Free Press
Dreyfus HL (1972) What computers can't do. Harper & Row Publishers, New York
Dreyfus HL (1992) What computers still can't do: a critique of artificial reason. The MIT Press, Cambridge
Ederer LS, Preston M (2011) The Innovation Design Protection and Piracy Prevention Act—fashion industry friend or faux? LexisNexis Communities Copyright and Trademark Law. https://www.lexisnexis.com/legalnewsroom/intellectual-property/b/copyright-trademark-law-blog/posts/the-innovative-design-protection-and-piracy-prevention-act-fashion-industry-friend-or-faux. Accessed 9 Sept 2022
European Commission (2020) Trends and developments in artificial intelligence. Challenges to the intellectual property rights framework. Publications Office of the European Union. https://op.europa.eu/en/publication-detail/-/publication/394345a1-2ecf-11eb-b27b-01aa75ed71a1/language-en. Accessed 17 Aug 2023
Federal Register (2023) Copyright registration guidance: works containing material generated by artificial intelligence, 16 Mar 2023. https://www.federalregister.gov/documents/2023/03/16/2023-05321/copyright-registration-guidance-works-containing-material-generated-by-artificial-intelligence. Accessed 17 Aug 2023
Financial Times (2023) Google invests $300mn in artificial intelligence start-up Anthropic, 3 Feb 2023. https://www.ft.com/content/583ead66-467c-4bd5-84d0-ed5df7b5bf9c. Accessed 16 Aug 2023
Fisher W (2001) Theories of intellectual property. In: Munzer S (ed) New essays in the legal and political theory of property. Cambridge University Press, Cambridge. https://cyber.harvard.edu/people/tfisher/iptheory.pdf. Accessed 30 Dec 2021
Fleck B, Baldock C (2003) Intellectual property protection for plant-related inventions in Europe. Nat Rev Genetics 4:834
Frankel S, Gervais D (eds) (2016) The internet and the emerging importance of new forms of intellectual property. Kluwer Law International, Boston
Frieder S, Pinchetti L, Chevalier A, Griffiths RR, Salvatori T, Lukasiewicz T, Petersen PC, Berner J (2023) Mathematical capabilities of ChatGPT. arXiv preprint. Submitted on 31 January 2023. https://arxiv.org/abs/2301.13867. Accessed 4 Aug 2023

Fromer JC (2012) Expressive incentives in intellectual property. Virginia Law Rev 98. https://law.stanford.edu/wp-content/uploads/sites/default/files/event/265497/media/slspublic/Expressive_Incentives_in_Intellectual_Property_1.pdf. Accessed 2 Jan 2022

Fryer WT III (1998) Vessel Hull Design Protection Act. Introductory report and legislative history resources. Fryer Institute on Intellectual Property Law. https://www.fryer.com/vhdparp.htm. Accessed 4 Sept 2022

Gallini N, Scotchmer S (2002) Intellectual property: when is it the best incentive system? Innov Policy Econ 2:51

Gaster JL (1996) The new EU directive concerning the legal protection of databases. Fordham Int. Law J 20:1129–1141

Gervais DJ (2007) The Protection of databases. Chicago-Kent Law Rev 82:1109

Gilbert R (2011) A world without intellectual property? Boldrin and Levine, Against Intellectual Monopoly'. J Econ Literat 49:421. https://escholarship.org/uc/item/3h7363s3. Accessed 3 Jan 2022

Ginsburg JC, Ali Budiardjo L (2019) Authors and machines. Berkeley Technol Law J 34:343

Goldstein B (2010) Sui Generis: a unique form of intellectual property governing compilations of data. AUTM Technol Transfer Practice Manual 3. https://www.autm.net/AUTMMain/media/ThirdEditionPDFs/V3/TTP_V3_P3_SuiGeneris.pdf. Accessed 27 Oct 2022

Goldstein P, Hugenholtz PB (2010) International copyright, 2nd edn. Oxford University Press, Oxford

Greenleaf G, Lindsay D (2018) Public rights: copyright's public domains. Cambridge University Press, Cambridge, p 192

Haroutunian-Gordon S (1988) Review: Mind over machine: a plea for the intuitive conception of mind. Educ Res 17:50

Heymann LA (2013) Overlapping intellectual property doctrines: election of rights versus selection of remedies. Stan Tech Law Rev 17:239

Hilty RM, Hoffmann J, Scheuerer S (2021) Intellectual property justification for artificial intelligence. In: Lee J-A, Hilty R, Liu K-C (eds) Artificial intelligence and intellectual property. Oxford University Press, Oxford

Hudson TB (1948) A brief history of the development of design patent protection in the United States. J Patent Off Soc 30:380

Hugenholtz PB (1998) Implementing the European database directive. In: Kabel JJC, Mom GJHM (eds) Intellectual property and information law, essays in honour of Herman Cohen Jehoram. Kluwer Law International, Boston

Hugenholtz PB (2019) Neighbouring rights are obsolete.https://link.springer.com/content/pdf/10.1007/s40319-019-00864-3.pdf. Accessed 27 Nov 2021

Intellectual Property Owners Association (2020) Sui Generis rights for trained AI models. https://ipo.org/wp-content/uploads/2020/11/SG-model-rights-committee-paper-pub.pdf. Accessed 16 Feb 2023

International Seed Federation. ISF view on intellectual property, adopted in Rio de Janeiro, Brazil, 28 June 2012. https://worldseed.org/wp-content/uploads/2015/10/View_on_Intellectual_Property_2012.pdf. Accessed 21 Dec 2022

Janis MD (2021) Second tier patent protection. Harvard Inte Law J 151. https://www.repository.law.indiana.edu/facpub/543/. Accessed 3 Nov 2021

Jimenez AVJT (2016) A Sui Generis System of protection for exceptionally original fashion designs. Loyola of Los Angeles Entertain Law Rev 36:101

Johns Hopkins Medicine. Q&A—What is intelligence? (discussion with Daeyeol Lee, 5 October 2020). https://www.hopkinsmedicine.org/news/articles/qa--what-is-intelligence. Accessed 1 Mar 2023

Karnell G (1991) The Nordic Catalogue Rule. In: Dommering EJ Hugenholtz PB (eds) Protecting works of fact. Kluwer Law and Taxation Publishers

Keebaugh RE (2005) Intellectual property and the protection of industrial design: are Sui Generis Protection measures the answer to vocal opponents and a Reluctant Congress? J Intellect Proper Law 13:255

Keller P (2022). A vanishing right? The Sui Generis database right and the proposed data act. Kluwer Copyright Blog, 4 Mar 2022. http://copyrightblog.kluweriplaw.com/2022/03/04/a-vanishing-right-the-sui-generis-database-right-and-the-proposed-data-act/. Accessed 31 July 2022

Kop M (2021) The right to process data for machine learning purposes in the EU. Harvard J Law Technol 34. https://jolt.law.harvard.edu/digest/the-right-to-process-data-for-machine-learning-purposes-in-the-eu. Accessed 20 Dec 2022

Lamiell JT (2003) Beyond individual and group differences: human individuality, scientific psychology, and William Stern's critical personalism. Sage Publications, London, p 62

Leaffer MA (2007) Database protection in the United States is alive and well: comments on Davison. Articl Maurer Faculty 2785:855

Legal review on industrial design protection in Europe. Under the contract with the Directorate General Internal Market, Industry, Entrepreneurship and SMEs (MARKT2014/083/D). Final Report—15 April 2016. https://op.europa.eu/en/publication-detail/-/publication/43fd4a5c-6c26-4639-ac9a-281ab57687de. Accessed 11 Sept 2022

Lemley MA (2000) Brief Amicus Curiae of Technology Law Professors: Ebay v. Bidder's Edge, No. 99-21200 in the U.S. District Court for the Northern District of California (100 F.Supp.2d 1058 (N.D. Cal. 2000))

Llewelyn M, Adcock M (2006) European plant intellectual property. Hart Publishing, Oxford

Lorenzoni I (2020) Artificial intelligence creates, invents … and challenges intellectual property law. Stockholm Intellect Proper Law Rev 3:26

Louwaars N, Engels J (2000) Intellectual property rights: patents or sui generis systems? In: Almekinders C, de Boef W (eds) Encouraging diversity. The conservation and development of plant genetic resources. Intermediate Technology Publications, p 279

Mahmood T (2015) Design law in the United States as compared to the European Community design system: what do we need to fix? Fordham Intellect Proper Media Entertain Law J 24:555

McCarthy J (2007) From here to human-level AI.Artif Intell 171:1174

McCarthy J (1996) Defending AI research: a collection of essays and reviews. CSLI Publications

McCarthy J, Minsky ML, Rochester N, Shannon CE (1955) A Proposal for the Dartmouth summer research project on artificial intelligence. http://jmc.stanford.edu/articles/dartmouth/dartmouth.pdf. Accessed 27 July 2023

McManis CR (2001) Database protection in the digital information age. Roger Williams Univ Law Rev 7

Merges RP (2011) Justifying intellectual property. Harvard University Press, Cambridge

Merrell C (2002) Trespass to Chattels in the age of the internet. Washington Univ Law Revi 80:675

Miko I (2008) Gregor Mendel and the principles of inheritance. Nat Educ 1(1):134. https://www.nature.com/scitable/topicpage/gregor-mendel-and-the-principles-of-inheritance-593/. Accessed 13 Oct 2022

Moore AD (1997) A Lockean theory of intellectual property. Hamline Law Rev 21:65

Moskvichev A, Odouard VV, Mitchell M (2023) The ConceptARC benchmark: evaluating understanding and generalization in the ARC Domain. arXiv preprint, submitted on 11 May 2023. https://arxiv.org/abs/2305.07141. Accessed 4 Aug 2023

Nicolas S, Andrieu B, Croizet JC, Sanitioso RB, Burman JT (2013) 'Sick? or slow? On the origins of intelligence as a psychological object. Intelligence 41:699

No Patents on Seeds! 'Correct legal interpretation of Article 53(b), EPC, regarding the patentability of essentially biological processes in relation to plants and animals within the context of the EU patent directive 98/44' (2021). https://www.no-patents-on-seeds.org/sites/default/files/news/Correct%20interpretation%20of%20Art.%2053(b).pdf. Accessed 14 Oct 2022

Olson BJ (2006) The Vessel Hull Design Protection Act of 1998: is it still afloat? J Intellect Proper Law Practice 1(11)

OpenAI. GPT-4 is OpenAI's most advanced system, producing safer and more useful responses. https://openai.com/gpt-4. Accessed 4 Aug 2023

Oriakhogba DO (2021) Dabus Gains Territory in South Africa and Australia: Revisiting the AI-inventorship question. South Afr Intellect Proper Law J 9:87

Oriola TA (2004) Electronic database protection and the limits of copyright: what options for developing countries. J World Intellect Proper 7:201

Patry WF (1994) Copyright law and practice. Bureau of National Affairs 1994. https://digital-law-online.info/patry/patry5.html#_ftnref90. Accessed 31 Jan 2022

Phillips J (2011) The great design conundrum. J Intellect Proper Law Practice 6(8):507

Phillips JC (1992) Sui generis intellectual property protection for computer software. George Washington Law Rev. https://cyber.harvard.edu/property/protection/resources/phillips_unedited.html. Accessed 27 Oct 2022

Publications Office of the European Union. Green Paper on Copyright and the Challenge Of Technology—Copyright Issues Requiring Immediate Action. Communication from The Commission. https://op.europa.eu/en/publication-detail/-/publication/a3392acf-2b75-11e7-9412-01aa75ed71a1/language-en/format-PDF/source-search. Accessed 8 July 2022

Purcell LE (2012–2013) A fashion flop: The Innovative Design Protection and Piracy Prevention Act (2012–2013). J Law Commerce 207:221–224

Quang J (2021) Does training AI violate copyright law? Berkeley Technol Law J 36:1407

Radomsky L (2000) Sixteen years after the passage of the U.S. semiconductor chip protection act: is international protection working?. Berkeley Technol Law J 15:1049

Raustiala K, Sprigman C (2006) The piracy paradox: innovation and intellectual property in fashion design. Virginia Law Rev 92:1687

Reichman JH (1994) Legal hybrids between the patent and copyright paradigms. Columbia Law Rev. 2432–2456. https://scholarship.law.duke.edu/faculty_scholarship/97/. Accessed 2 Nov 2021

Reichman JH (1995). Universal minimum standards of intellectual property protection under the TRIPS component of the WTO agreement. International Lawyer 29:345–348. https://scholarship.law.duke.edu/cgi/viewcontent.cgi?article=1617&context=faculty_scholarship. Accessed 4 Jan 2022

Ricketson S, Ginsburg J (2022) International copyright and neighbouring rights. The Berne convention and beyond. Oxford University Press, Oxford

Seay NS (1993) Intellectual property in plants. In: Baenziger PS, Kleese RA, Barnes RF (eds) Intellectual property rights: protection of plant materials. Crop Science Society of America, New York, p 61

Smith BC (2019) The promise of artificial intelligence. Reckoning and judgment, vol xv. The MIT Press, Cambridge

Stanford Encyclopedia of Philosophy. Intellectual Property. https://plato.stanford.edu/entries/intellectual-property/. Accessed 7 Jan 2022

Stanford University. Gathering strength, gathering storms: the one hundred year study on artificial intelligence (AI100) 2021 Study Panel Report. https://ai100.stanford.edu/gathering-strength-gathering-storms-one-hundred-year-study-artificial-intelligence-ai100-2021-study. Accessed 3 Aug 2023

Stern W (1914) The psychological methods of testing intelligence (Guy M. Whipple, trans.). Warwick & York, Inc., New York

Suthersanen U (2011) Function, art and fashion: do we need the EU design law? Queen Mary School of Law Legal Studies Research Paper No. 88. https://papers.ssrn.com/sol3/papers.cfm?abstract_id=1945142. Accessed 2 Nov 2021

Suthersanen U (2018) Utility models: do they really serve national innovation strategies? Queen Mary School of Law Legal Studies Research Paper No. 274. https://papers.ssrn.com/sol3/papers.cfm?abstract_id=3139963. Accessed 4 Nov 2021

Suthersanen U (2019) Utility models: do they really serve national innovation strategies? In: Drexl J, Sanders AK (eds) The innovation society and intellectual property, vol 2.

Edward Elgar, Cheltenham. https://www.elgaronline.com/view/edcoll/9781789902341/9781789902341.00010.xml. Accessed 12 Jan 2022
Swansea University. 2019 Loebner Prize. https://www.swansea.ac.uk/computational-foundry/news/mitsuku-wins2019loebner-prize/. Accessed 27 July 2023
Terman LM (1916) The measurement of intelligence. An explanation of and a complete guide for the use of the stanford revision and extension of the Binet-Simon intelligence scale. In: Cubberley EP (ed) Riverside textbooks in education 2007. The Riverside Press. https://www.gutenberg.org/files/20662/20662-h/20662-h.htm#CHAPTER_VIII. Accessed 7 Mar 2023
The Role of Data in AI (2020) Report for the Data Governance Working Group of the Global Partnership of AI. Digital Curation Centre. Trilateral Research. School of Informatics, the University of Edinburgh, Nov 2020. https://gpai.ai/projects/data-governance/role-of-data-in-ai.pdf. Accessed 8 Aug 2023
Turing AM (1950) Computing machinery and intelligence. Mind Quart Rev Phycol Philos Lix(236):433
U.S. Copyright Office and USPTO (2023) The Vessel Hull Design Protection Act: overview and analysis. https://www.copyright.gov/reports/vhdpa-report.pdf. Accessed 22 Dec 2022
U.S. Copyright Office, Compendium of U.S. Copyright Office Practices § 101 (3rd edn., 2021)
UPOV Press Release No. 8 'Diplomatic Conference for the revision of the International Convention for the Protection of New Varieties of Plants', Geneva, 21 Mar 1991. https://www.upov.int/edocs/pressdocs/en/upov_pr_008.pdf. Accessed 13 Oct 2022
Van Brunt J (1985) Ex parte Hibberd: another landmark decision. Nat Biotechnol 3:1059
Von Holstein P (1967) International Co-operation in the Field of Patent Law with special reference to the Activities of the Council of Europe. Int Comp Law Quart 16(1):191
WIPO. Frequently asked questions: AI and IP policy. What is artificial intelligence? https://www.wipo.int/about-ip/en/artificial_intelligence/faq.html. Accessed 27 Feb 2023
WIPO (2022) Standing Committee on Copyright and Related Rights. Seventh Session, Geneva, 13–17 May 2002. Study on the Protection of Unoriginal Databases. https://www.wipo.int/edocs/mdocs/copyright/en/sccr_7/sccr_7_3.pdf. Accessed 20 Dec 2022
Würtenberger G, Ekvad M, Kooij P, Kiewiet B (2021) European Union plant variety protection. Oxford University Press, Oxford
Zohn W (2018) Examining the role of patent quality in large-scale "Patent War" litigation. A historical comparison and proposal for a restorative U.S. Patent System (Nomos Verlagsgesellschaft mbH 2018). https://www.jstor.org/stable/j.ctv941rps.9. Accessed 9 Sept 2022

Legislation

Act on Copyright in Literary and Artistic Works of Sweden (1960)
Berne Convention for the Protection of Literary and Artistic Works (as amended on September 28, 1979). https://wipolex.wipo.int/en/treaties/textdetails/12214. Accessed 22 Nov 2021
Commission of the European Communities. Green Paper on the legal protection of industrial design. Working document of the services of the Commission. III/F/5131/91-EN, June 1991
Commission Regulation (EC) 2245/2002 of 21 October 2002 implementing Council Regulation (EC) 6/2002 on Community designs [2002] OJ L341/28
Commission Regulation (EC) 2246/2002 of 16 December 2002 on the fees payable to the Office for Harmonization in the Internal Market (Trade Marks and Designs) in respect of the registration of Community designs [2002] OJ L341/54
Communication from the Commission to the European Parliament, the Council, the European Economic and Social Committee and the Committee of the Regions. A European strategy for data. COM/2020/66 final
Computer Fraud and Abuse Act (1986) 18 U.S.C. § 1030
Copyright Act (1909) 35 Stat. 1075

Copyright Act (1976) 90 Stat. 2541
Copyright Act of 31 May 1790, ch. 15, 1 Stat. 124
Council Decision of 30 May 2005, approving the accession of the European Community to the International Convention for the Protection of New Varieties of Plants, as revised in Geneva on 19 March 1991 [2005] OJ L192
Council Regulation (EC) 2100/94 of 27 July 1994 on Community plant variety rights [1994] OJ L227/1
Council Regulation (EC) No 6/2002 of 12 December 2001 on Community designs [2001] OJ 3/1
Design Piracy Prohibition Act. H.R.2033—110th Congress (2007–2008)
Design Piracy Prohibition Act. H.R.2196—111th Congress (2009–2010)
Design Privacy Prohibition Acts S.1957 — 110th Congress (2007–2008)
Digital Millennium Copyright Act (1998) 112 Stat. 2860
Directive (EU) 2019/1024 of the European Parliament and of the Council of 20 June 2019 on open data and the re-use of public sector information [2019] OJ L172/56
Directive (EU) 2019/790 of the European Parliament and of the Council of 17 April 2019 on copyright and related rights in the Digital Single Market and amending Directives 96/9/EC and 2001/29/EC [2019] OJ L130/92
Directive 2001/29/EC of the European Parliament and of the Council of 22 May 2001 on the harmonisation of certain aspects of copyright and related rights in the information society [2001] OJ L167
Directive 2006/115/EC of the European Parliament and of the Council of 12 December 2006 on rental right and lending right and on certain rights related to copyright in the field of intellectual property [2006] OJ L376/28
Directive 2006/116/EC of the European Parliament and of the Council of 12 December 2006 on the term of protection of copyright and certain related rights [2006] OJ L 372
Directive 96/9/EC of 11 March 1996 on the legal protection of databases [1996] OJ L 77/20
Directive 98/44/EC of the European Parliament and of the Council of 6 July 1998 on the legal protection of biotechnological inventions [1998] OJ L213/13
Directive 98/71/EC of the European Parliament and of the Council of 13 October 1998 on the legal protection of designs [1998] OJ L 289/28
European Parliament. P9_TA(2023)0236. Artificial Intelligence Act. Amendments adopted by the European Parliament on 14 June 2023 on the proposal for a regulation of the European Parliament and of the Council on laying down harmonized rules on artificial intelligence (Artificial Intelligence Act) and amending certain Union legislative acts (COM(2021)0206—C9-0146/2021—2021/0106(COD)). https://www.europarl.europa.eu/doceo/document/TA-9-2023-0236_EN.pdf. Accessed 14 Aug 2023
European Patent Office. The European Patent Convention. https://www.epo.org/law-practice/legal-texts/html/epc/2016/e/ar53.html. Accessed 2 Oct 2022
H.R. 3261—Database and Collections of Information Misappropriation Act. 108th Congress (2003–2004)
H.R.1858—Consumer and Investor Access to Information Act of 1999. 106th Congress (1999–2000)
H.R.2652 - Collections of Information Antipiracy Act. 105th Congress (1997–1998)
H.R.3531—Database Investment and Intellectual Property Antipiracy Act of 1996. 104th Congress (1995–1996)
H.R.354—Collections of Information Antipiracy Act. 106th Congress (1999–2000)
H.R.3872—Consumer Access to Information Act of 2004. 108th Congress (2003–2004)
Innovative Design Protection Act. S.3523—112th Congress (2011–2012)
Innovative Design Protection and Piracy Prevention Act. H.R.2511—112th Congress (2011–2012)
International Convention for the Protection of Performers, Producers of Phonograms and Broadcasting Organisations. Rome, 26 October 1961. https://treaties.un.org/pages/ViewDetails.aspx?src=TREATY&mtdsg_no=XIV-3&chapter=14&clang=_en. Accessed 20 Feb 2023
Lanham Act (1946) 15 U.S. Code § 1125

Plant Patent Act (1930) 35 U.S.C. Ch. 15 Section 161
Plant Variety Protection Act (1970) 7 U.S.C. §§ 2321–2582
Procedure 1992/0393/COD. COM (1992) 24: Proposal for a Council Directive on the legal protection of databases. https://eur-lex.europa.eu/procedure/EN/1992_393. Accessed 14 July 2022
Proposal for a Council Directive on the Legal Protection of Databases, COM (92)24 final [1992] OJ 1992 C156/4
Proposal for a European Parliament and Council Directive on the legal protection of designs 1993/0464/COD
Proposal for a European Parliament and Council Regulation on the Community Design. COM/93/342FINAL - COD 463
Regulation (EU) 2022/868 of the European Parliament and of the Council of 30 May 2022 on European data governance and amending Regulation (EU) 2018/1724 (Data Governance Act) [2022] OJ L 152/1
Regulation (EU) 2023/2854 of the European Parliament and of the Council of 13 December 2023 on harmonised rules on fair access to and use of data and amending Regulation (EU) 2017/2394 and Directive (EU) 2020/1828 (Data Act) [2023] OJ L2023/2854
Semiconductor Chip Protection Act (1984) 98 Stat. 3335
Swedish Statute Book, SFS, 1960:729
Title 17 of the United States Code
Title 35 of the United States Code
Treaty establishing the European Community (Consolidated version 2002) [2002] OJ C 325
U.S. Constitution Article I § 8 Clause 8
United Nations Human Rights Office of the High Commissioner. International Covenant on Civil and Political Rights. https://www.ohchr.org/en/instruments-mechanisms/instruments/international-covenant-civil-and-political-rights. Accessed 11 Aug 2023
United Nations Human Rights Office of the High Commissioner. Universal Declaration of Human Rights. https://www.ohchr.org/en/human-rights/universal-declaration/translations/english. Accessed 11 Aug 2023
WIPO and BIRPI. Model Law for developing countries on industrial designs. https://www.wipo.int/edocs/pubdocs/en/wipo_pub_808.pdf. Accessed 19 Aug 2022
WIPO Performances and Phonograms Treaty (1996). https://www.wipo.int/treaties/en/ip/wppt/. Accessed 21 Aug 2023
WTO. Agreement on trade related aspects of intellectual property rights, including trade in counterfeit goods. https://www.wto.org/english/docs_e/legal_e/27-trips_01_e.htm. Accessed 4 Jan 2022

Table of Cases

AB Volvo v Erik Veng (UK) Ltd (Case C-238/87) [1988] ECR 06211
Andersen v. Stability AI Ltd., 3:23-cv-00201, (N.D. Cal.)
Bonito Boats Inc. v. Thunder Craft Boats Inc. 489 U.S. 141 (1989)
Case No. CV997654HLHVBKX (C.D. Cal. Mar. 7, 2003)
CCC Information Services v. Maclean Hunter Market Reports, Inc. 44 F.3d 61 (2d Cir. 1994)
Cofemel - Sociedade de Vestuário, SA v G-Star Raw CV (Case C-683/17) [2019] Court Reports – general
Consorzio italiano della componentistica di ricambio per autoveicoli and Maxicar v Régie nationale des usines Renault (Case C-53/87) [1988] ECR 06039
Diamond v. Chakrabarty 447 U.S. 303 (1980)
Door-Master Corporation v. Yorktowne, Inc., 256 F.3d 1308, 1312–13 (Fed. Cir. 2001)
eBay v. Bidder's Edge 100 F. Supp. 2d 1058 (N.D. Cal. 2000)

EF Cultural Travel BV v. Explorica, Inc., 274 F.3d 577 (1st Cir. 2001)
Endstra v. Uitgerverij Nieuw Amsterdam Supreme Court of the Netherlands C07/131h (2008)
Ex parte Hibberd 227 U.S.P.Q. 443 (P.T.O. Bd. App. & Inter. 1985)
Feist Publications, Inc. v. Rural Telephone Service Co., Inc. U.S. Supreme Court 111 S.Ct. 1282 (1991) (discussed in more detail in Part II of this research paper)
Feist Publications, Inc. v. Rural Telephone Service Co., Inc. U.S. Supreme Court 111 S.Ct. 1282 (1991)
Fixtures Marketing Limited v. AB Svenska Spel (Case C-338/02) [2004] ECR I-10497
Fixtures Marketing Ltd v. Organismos prognostikon agonon podosfairou AE (OPAP) (Case C-444/02) [2004] ECR I-10549
Fixtures Marketing Ltd v. Oy Veikkaus Ab (Case C-46/02) [2004] ECR I-10365
Gorham Company v. White 81 U.S. (14 Wall.) 511 (1872)
Infopaq International A/S v Danske Dagblades Forening (Case C-5/08) [2009] ECR I-06569
Intel Corp. v. Hamidi 71 P.3d 296 (Cal. 2003)
International News Service v. Associated Press, 248 U.S. 215 (1918)
J 8/20 (Designation of inventor/DABUS) 21-12-2021
J 9/20 (Designation of inventor/DABUS II) 21-12-2021
J. E. M. Ag Supply, Inc. v. Pioneer Hi-Bred International, Inc.534 U.S. 124 (2001)
Kadrey v. Meta Platforms, Inc., 3:23-cv-03417, (N.D. Cal.)
Keurkoop BV v Nancy Kean Gifts BV (Case C-144/81) [1982] ECR 02853
Key Publications, Inc. v. Chinatown Today Publishing Enterprises Inc. 945 F.2d 509 (2d Cir. 1991)
Kieselstein-Cord v. Accessories by Pearl, Inc. 632 F.2d 989 (1980)
Kingdom of the Netherlands v European Parliament and Council of the European Union (Case C-377/98) [2001] ECR I-07079
Kregos v. Associated Press 937 F.2d 700 (2d Cir. 1991)
L. v. Alphabet Inc., 3:23-cv-03440, (N.D. Cal.)
Mazer v. Stein 347 U.S. 201 (1954)
P.M. v. OpenAI LP, 3:23-cv-03199, (N.D. Cal.)
Peters v. Active Manufacturing Co. 129 U.S. 530, 9 S. Ct. 389 (1889)
Pioneer Hi-Bred International v. Holden Foundation Seeds, Inc., 35 F.3d 1226 (1994)
Pioneer Hi-Bred International. Inc. v. Holden Foundation Seeds, Inc. No. 81-60-E slip op. S.D. Iowa, Oct. 29, 1987
Pollster v. Gigmania, Ltd. 170 F. Supp. 2d 974 (E.D. Cal. 2000)
ProCD v. Zeidenberg 86 F.3d 1447
re Application No. 16/524,350, Decision on Petition, 22 April 2020. https://www.uspto.gov/sites/default/files/documents/16524350_22apr2020.pdf. Accessed 17 August 2023
Register.com v. Verio 356 F.3d 393 (2d Cir. 2004)
Seiko Epson Corporation v. Nu-Kote International, Inc. 190 F.3d 1360, 1368 (Fed. Cir. 1999)
Silverman v. OpenAI, Inc., 3:23-cv-03416, (N.D. Cal.)
Star Athletica, LLC v. Varsity Brands, Inc. 580 U.S. ___ (2017)
T1054/96 'Plants/NOVARTIS' [1998] OJ EPO 511
The British Horseracing Board Ltd and Others v. William Hill Organisation Ltd (Case C-203/02) [2004] ECR I-10415
Thrifty-Tel v. Bezenek, 46 Cal. App. 4th 1559, 1566, 54 Cal. Rptr. 2d 468 (1996)
Tremblay v. OpenAI, Inc., 3:23-cv-03223, (N.D. Cal.)
Two Pesos, Inc. v. Taco Cabana, Inc. 505 U.S. 763 (1992)
Van Dale Lexicografie B.V. v. Rudolf Jan Romme Supreme Court of the Netherlands NJ 1991/608 (1991)
Wal-Mart Stores, Inc. v. Samara Brothers, Inc., 529 U.S. 205, 120 S. Ct. 1339 (2000)

Index

I. Kazeeva, *Sui Generis Intellectual Property Protection*, Perspectives in Law, Business and Innovation, https://doi.org/10.1007/978-981-99-8897-6

The manufacturer's authorised representative in the EU is Springer Nature Customer Service Centre GmbH, Europaplatz 3, 69115 Heidelberg, Germany. If you have any concerns regarding our products, please contact ProductSafety@springernature.com

Printed and bound by CPI Group (UK) Ltd, Croydon, CR0 4YY
01/10/2026
02225876-0001